Presented To:

_____

From:

_____

Date:

_____

PRAYER CHANGES THINGS

DESTINY IMAGE BOOKS BY BENI JOHNSON

The Happy Intercessor

The Joy of Intercession

Beautiful One with Heidi Baker et al

Experiencing the Heavenly Realm with Judy Franklin

Walking in the Supernatural with Bill Johnson et al

INCLUDED IN THIS IN-DEPTH AND INSIGHTFUL BOOK
ARE EXCERPTS FROM THE FOLLOWING
BOOKS AND AUTHORS:

The Prayer God Loves to Answer by Don Nori Sr.

Prayer Storm by James W. Goll

The Happy Intercessor by Beni Johnson

How God Answers Prayer by Elmer L. Towns

How to Pray by Morris Cerullo

Praying to Change Your Life by Suzette T. Caldwell

Prayer in Another Dimension by Sue Curran

The Hidden Power of Prayer and Fasting by Mahesh Chavda

Praying With Power by C. Peter Wagner

PRAYER CHANGES THINGS

*Taking Your Life to
the Next Prayer Level*

COMPILED *by* BENI JOHNSON

DESTINY IMAGE® PUBLISHERS, INC.

P.O. Box 310, Shippensburg, PA 17257-0310

"Promoting Inspired Lives."

This book and all other Destiny Image, Revival Press, MercyPlace, Fresh Bread, Destiny Image Fiction, and Treasure House books are available at Christian bookstores and distributors worldwide.

For a U.S. bookstore nearest you, call 1-800-722-6774.

For more information on foreign distributors, call 717-532-3040.

Reach us on the Internet: www.destinyimage.com.

ISBN 13 TP: 978-0-7684-0299-5

ISBN 13 Ebook: 978-0-7684-8790-9

For Worldwide Distribution, Printed in the U.S.A.

1 2 3 4 5 6 7 8 / 16 15 14 13 12

CONTENTS

INTRODUCTION

At Bethel in Redding, where we pastor, we have a ministry school. One day while teaching on intercession and prayer, I ended the session and opened it up for questions. One of our young men said, "I don't feel like I fit into the whole intercession thing." My response was, "Wait, what do you think you are doing when we get you up on the stage to dance?" You see, this young man had an amazing ability to dance in a warlike dance to bring a spiritual change to the atmosphere. I told him that when he did that, things happened in the spirit realm. Then I told the whole class that there are many ways to pray and move in intercession, that it's not always about words, and that God uses our gifts for intercession.

At Bethel Church every Saturday we have what we call Healing Rooms. People come from all over the world to this place to receive prayer for healing. One of the things that people do first when they come to the Healing Rooms is to sit and soak in the presence of God. We have live worship and our prophetic artists painting in one of the rooms, which we call the Encounter

Room, and as the people wait to receive prayer, they sit in the room and get all saturated in the presence of God.

One of our prophetic intercessors, who happens to be an artist/painter, placed one of her paintings in our Healing Room one day. A lady walked up to that beautiful painting with the word *hope* on it, and stood in front of it and began to cry. Here is the account of the amazing healing that resulted:

On October 17, 2009, at the Healing Rooms, Tom[1] had called out a word of knowledge in the Encounter Room for a problem with the back of the head (which is where a woman had a cancerous tumor). Tom prayed and the woman said nothing happened. Tom just encouraged her to keep getting prayer and that God was going to do something. Later on, Dan called out a word of knowledge for tumors, and he also went to pray for her. When he was there, she told him that when Tom had prayed for her, she was healed of tunnel vision (which she never even mentioned that she had).

Kathy, who also ministers in the Healing Rooms, spoke to her, and she told Kathy the doctors had said her situation was "hopeless," so Kathy took her into the Healing Room and showed her the painting that one of the artists had painted, on which was written the word, "Hope." She broke down in tears as she looked at it, and God resurrected hope in her heart.

Then she returned to the Encounter Room, and two men took her and her fiancé over and she told them the doctors had said she had only two months to live and her cancer was inoperable. They declared *life* and touched her. She said the pain and pressure were suddenly gone, and as they were praising God, she cried out and grabbed her ear. She asked for a napkin as it was seriously draining. One of the men got her some tissues. Incidentally, her fiancé had shaking of the hands, arthritis in his wrists, and lower back pain. They asked him how he was doing, and he couldn't find any of those things anymore! The next day at church he still had no more problems with those things, and she said she had stopped taking the morphine as there was no more pain. She had no withdrawals from morphine, either.

Thursday she e-mailed and said the tumor had been the size of a golf ball and had shrunk to the size of a plum pit and had no fluid in it, and the doctors said they could find no cancer cells in her. Praise Jesus![2]

God's first language is not English nor is it any other language. When it comes to prayer and intercession, words are important but not necessary. I believe when that lady stood in front of that painting, it released in her hope and it released healing.

In this book the verse in James 5 is mentioned a few times.

> *Confess your trespasses to one another, and pray for one another, that you may be healed. The effective, fervent prayer of a righteous man avails much* (James 5:16).

This verse has for me been a verse of much thought and meditation, especially the last part of the verse. I have looked it up in many translations and thought about what it could mean. Let me give you a few of those translations, and then we will study this more.

> *The earnest* (heartfelt, continued) *prayer of a righteous man makes tremendous power available [dynamic in its working].* (AMP)

The insistent prayer of a righteous person is power-fully effective. (The Eastern/Greek Orthodox Bible, EOB)

For the power of the prayer which a righteous person prays is great. (The Original Aramaic New Testament in Plain English)

Two things stand out to me as important in the last part of this verse: 1) being a righteous person and 2) effective prayers get the job done. To me being righteous plays a very important role in causing our prayers to be effective, or, as the Amplified version says so beautifully, "dynamic in its working."

In Matthew 5, we find the fourth beatitude talks of righteousness:

Blessed are those who hunger and thirst after righteousness, for they shall be filled.

The Greek word for "righteous" is *dikalos,* and the Greek word for "righteousness" is *dikaiousyne.* The Hebrew word for "righteousness" is *sedaqa. Sedaqa* denotes "a relationship."[3] This seems to say to us that being righteous has to do with being in relationship. Van Rod in *Old Testament Theology* writes that "from the earliest times Israel celebrated Jahweh as the one who bestowed on His people the all embracing gift of His righteousness and this *tsdqh (righteousness)* bestowed on Israel is always a saving gift."[4]

Being in right relationship with God is what I've always heard was the definition of being righteous. Being righteous is all about being in a relationship with our Lord. It's not just having the Lord but knowing Him. I have my husband as my husband because we are married, but I also have a relationship with him because I spend time with him. I know him. I can just be saved, which will get me to heaven, but I long for that righteous relationship with my God, to know him more and more! That is longing for righteousness.

See, when I know God as much as I can and He knows me so much more, there is a power in that. There is some real authority that happens. There is trust that happens. I can trust God, and He can trust me. The idea of God trusting me enough to tell me His secrets is all I need to get my prayers going in the right direction. That one thought, "that God can trust me" turns my world upright.

The more we seek after righteousness, the more our prayers will be effective. I don't want lifeless prayers. I want prayers that will change the world. When I pray, I want to know that I am making a difference. Seeking after righteousness will accomplish that.

The psalmist writes in Psalm 17:15, *As for me, I will see Your face in righteousness; I shall be satisfied when I awake in Your likeness.*

The Amplified Bible reads, *As for me, I will continue beholding Your face in righteousness (rightness, justice, and right standing with You); I shall be fully satisfied, when I awake [to find myself] beholding Your form [and having sweet communion with You].*

And, the Rotherham's Emphasized Bible reads, *I in righteousness shall behold thy face, shall be satisfied when awakened by a vision of thee.*

I believe that when we stand before God in rightness, justice and right standing with God, we will see Him. And in seeing Him, we will understand His ways and see what He is doing. Then, as we petition Father with our prayers, those prayers can be nothing but effective.

I like to experiment with prayer and try new things to see what will work.

I was texting with a friend who was telling me that she was ministering to a guy who was a royal in a cult. She asked for some prayer in the matter. I told her I would pray. I began praying, and I got an idea. Both my friend and I could feel that God was all over this, and I knew it was just a matter of time. Because I am a tweeter on Twitter, a social network accessed by phone or computer, I decided to befriend this young man to get an idea of what he was about. I do believe in being informed about things so I can pray better. So, I befriended him. When I saw his tweet come up on my phone, I got this idea, "I'm going to pray for him every time I see his tweet."

So that's what I did, but I decided to say the first thing that would come to my head and pray that for him. It was really fun. As the week went by there were many tweets, and I would just speak out the first thing that would come to my head, simple things like, "God you are so after him" or "God get him; bring him to you." One day he posted a verse, and I knew at that point he was close. Sure enough the next day my friend let me know that he had come to the Lord. A group of Holy Ghost young people who had just come from one of our gatherings for the weekend went back home and got a hold of him. This young man saw the extreme change in these young people and couldn't help but jump right into God.

Many times when I am teaching on prayer, I will have people wait before God, and then in the waiting, I will have them re-ask God about a request they have been praying for. Sometimes we need the fresh wind of God on our prayers that will make them more effective. But we first need to behold God. In waiting, we look at Him and not the problem or request. We abide in Him; then in turn He abides in us. That's when the fresh wind of God can blow on us.

I have enjoyed reading each chapter in the compilation book, the creativity and each person's thoughts on prayer and what makes it work for them. Whether it's using the word or fasting or soaking or when the travail of the Lord comes on your spirit, whatever the tool, there is a right standing before God that ties it all together. That makes the prayers work.

One more thought on being righteous before God. Isaiah 32:17 reads:

> *And the work of righteousness shall be peace; and the effect of righteousness quietness and assurance for ever.*

One of the fruits of righteousness is peace. I believe that it's very important to pray out of a place of peace. If we are in right standing with God in relationship (righteous), we will have that peace from heaven. And when we pray from a place of peace and not fear, we will see fruit. If fear comes, we *must* step back, take a breath of heaven, and find our peace and pray from there. The Bible says, *Do not be afraid of sudden terror, Nor of trouble from the wicked when it comes* (Prov. 3:25).

Seated right with God in relationship, we are seated in the heavenly realm and can see from His vantage point. There is not terror from there. Praying from fear only puts us in a place of having to control. It makes you feel like you are the only one who can change the circumstance and brings on stress, anxiousness and striving, which gets you nowhere. When praying, check yourself and see if you are praying from fear or peace? Am I in right standing with God?

There are times when prayer is like being in labor and having a baby. It takes work and lots of focus. I've been in on many births and prayed through many of them. One of the things a woman must understand is that her body will work best during labor if she can focus on being peaceful and not getting afraid. When our daughter, Leah, went through her first labor experience. I was her coach. Being the coach, I was right in her face the whole time, coaching her into every contraction. At one point towards the end, I noticed that she was getting really anxious and fearful. The thought came to me to speak peace to her as she started each contraction. It was amazing how that worked. As we spoke peace, the *Shalom* of heaven, you could feel it come once again. Over and over, we spoke it until that baby was born.

It is the same with our prayers. We must be focused and sitting in a place of peace, in heavenly places, and praying from a place of peace. Find God, and you find peace. Find peace, and you will find the answer.

As you read through these chapters, be reminded once again that God uses our gifts and our personalities, and regardless of our experiences in prayer, we all have one thing in common: God and our relationship with Him are what bring us into this great ministry of prayer.

Endnotes

1. The names of the people have been changed.

2. http://www.ibethel.org/testimonies/2009/10/27/ healed-of-brain-cancer

3. Jesus through Middle Eastern Eyes. Pg.80 (as quoted in Old Testament Theology by Von Rad)

4. (Jesus through Middle Eastern Eyes. Pg. 78 (as quoted in Old Testament Theology by Von Rad)

Chapter I

LET YOUR YES BE YES

by Don Nori, Sr.

*Now this is the confidence that we have in Him,
that if we ask anything according to His will,
He hears us. And if we know that He hears us,
whatever we ask, we know that we have the petitions
that we have asked of Him* (1 John 5:14-15).

In *How to Obtain Fullness of Power*, E.M. Bounds writes, "There are many people greatly puzzled because their prayers never seem to reach the ear of God, but fall back, unanswered, to the earth. There is no mystery about it. It is because they have not met the one great, fundamental condition of prevailing prayer—a surrendered will and a surrendered life. It is when we make God's will ours, that He makes our will His."

This what Jesus means when He tells us to let our yes be yes. This is vitally important teaching from the heart of our Master. It is clear that He wants us to say yes to Him, but our yes needs to be far more than just lip service; it must be the central focus of our lives. For our yes to be yes, it must be lived and believed, not just spoken, and our lives and wills must be surrendered fully to Him.

So, yes is far more than just a word. Indeed, it is more than just a prayer. It is a lifestyle commitment and an attitude of heart that perseveres in agreement with God and His dream for you, no matter what the negative people and negative circumstances around you might declare.

> *You must be strong in believing that God will always do what's best for you.*

To let your yes be yes, you must be strong in believing that God will always do what's best for you. As a yes believer, you will walk by faith, not by sight, always trusting in the Lord, seeking to abide in His presence, and endeavoring to follow the dream He has for you.

There are really only two responses to God and His will; they are either yes or no. There is no middle ground, no gray area. You either affirm the will of God in your life, or you deny Him and His will. Even when you do not understand what the will of God is, your willingness to agree with His will opens the doors of opportunity and possibility that can come in no other way.

I know that there are some who insist that you must know the will of God before you can trust Him for it. But that is only true when you do not believe God has only His best ready for you.

When you begin to understand that God's dream is the happiest, the most fulfilled, and the most effective life you can live, it will become easier to rest in Him, especially when you don't have a real clue about His plans for you.

WE ARE "UNDER CONSTRUCTION"

When you say yes to the Lord, your life becomes a cleared building site—His property, if you will. In other words, you are under construction. He has purchased you so that He might be able to live within you and build His Kingdom in you and through you. To Him, therefore, you are valuable "real estate."

When you allow yourself to be His building site, you will then be willing for Him to clear your heart, gently and lovingly removing all those things that are no longer important to you or Him. He is preparing a habitation for Himself within you.

Paul writes, *"Or do you not know that your body is the temple of the Holy Spirit who is in you, whom you have from God, and you are not your own? For you were bought at a price; therefore glorify God in your body and in your spirit, which are God's"* (1 Cor. 6:19-20).

When you say "yes" to God, you do not belong to yourself any longer. You are purposefully laying aside your will, believing that His will is far better than yours. You are embracing His dream for you. You are His, and, as His possession, He can now begin the most exciting time of your life. He is now beginning to build you and to lead you into your destiny.

For Him to build His Kingdom within you, God understandably removes all existing structures that you had built while you were constructing your own personal kingdom. He will clear the landscape of your heart, leaving it completely bare, ready to have His foundation and building put on your site. He will mercifully go deep into your life so as to remove everything that's old, decaying, and useless. Even the old foundation upon which your life was built may need to be adjusted or even removed so it can be rebuilt in His way and according to His dream for you.

He wants to build a house of His own choosing, a building not made with human hands, but one in which He will live and give you true fulfillment every day of your life. His work is always powerful and unique. In a very real sense, we are still being fearfully and wonderfully made!

> *You are still being fearfully and wonderfully made!*

GOD-POSSESSED

The Holy Spirit lives within you. This means that you are a God-possessed person.

As such, God is calling you to a higher place in the Spirit, a place where you can hear His voice, experience an ever-deepening faith, and enjoy His providence, favor, and provision wherever you are.

This is the Most Holy Place that I referred to earlier—the place where you will have fellowship with the Father and hear Him speaking to you, waiting for you to respond in full surrender with His will.

I remember a time when Jonathan and Donald, my two oldest sons, were seven and five years old, and their mother was in the kitchen baking chocolate chip cookies. The boys were watching her, as she pulled the freshly baked treats out of the oven.

I'm sure the boys were enjoying the sight and smell of the cookies, and they were surely anticipating their taste. Cathy put the baking tray on the counter and said, "Don't touch the cookies, Boys. They are too hot!"

"OK, Mommy!" they said.

She stepped out of the kitchen for a moment, and the boys headed right to the cookies! Needless to say, they burnt their fingertips and began to cry. It was a lesson they needed to learn only once, for the next time Cathy made cookies, she pulled the tray out of the oven, and Jonathan asked, "Are the trays hot?"

"Yes, very hot," she replied.

"Will you tell me when they're cool enough?" was his next question.

Jonathan and Donald had learned their lesson, but it was a hard, pain-filled lesson that would not have been necessary had they simply listened to their mother's voice and responded with a true yes from their hearts. They had said yes, but they did not truly mean it. In actuality, their yes had been a no.

> ***In actuality, their yes had been a no.***

When we say "yes" to the Father, we must do so with a willing heart, one that wants to do what He tells us to do.

Paul writes, *"I beseech you therefore, brethren, by the mercies of God, that you present your bodies a living sacrifice, holy, acceptable to God, which is your reasonable service. And do not be conformed to this world, but be transformed by the renewing of your mind, that you may prove what is that good and acceptable and perfect will of God"* (Rom. 12:1-2).

Presenting your whole life to God as a living sacrifice is truly a reasonable service to Him in light of all His mercies to you. Offering yourself to Him completely is a resounding yes to Him that is heard throughout Heaven. It reaches His heart with the sweetness of honey and the innocence of a newborn child. It is then that you will discover and begin to live His perfectly wonderful dream for your life.

WEAKNESS DOES NOT DISQUALIFY

You must never allow your human weakness to disqualify you for what God has planned for you. Your failures do not prove that you are wicked; they simply prove that you are human. Though you are filled with God, it's important to remember that you are a human being who is filled with God.

That's why you need to enter and stay in the yes of God, for there you will be refined, strengthened, healed, taught, and made whole in every way.

Run *to* God, not *away* from Him, when you fail. Paul said, *"And He said to me, 'My grace is sufficient for you, for My strength is made perfect in weakness.' Therefore most gladly I will rather boast in my infirmities, that the power of Christ may rest upon me. Therefore I take pleasure in infirmities, in reproaches, in needs, in persecutions, in distresses, for Christ's sake. For when I am weak, then I am strong"* (2 Cor. 12:9-10).

Paul was a man who knew he had weaknesses, but he used his weaknesses as a sign that he had to run to the Lord for strength. Religion, on the other hand, causes people to run away from God when they fail, due to guilt and shame. God, however, wants us to run to Him, so He can continue His work in our lives.

WEAKNESS OR STRENGTH?

How could Paul make such a statement as this: "When I am weak, then I am strong"? It doesn't seem to make much sense, does it? But the answer is simple. The weakest part of Paul became the strongest part of him because he confessed his weakness and asked the Lord to make it strong. Over time, therefore, his weak points became his strong points.

Weakness and failure never stopped Paul. What they did was teach him to pray. He did not allow weakness to disqualify him for what God had in store for him. He chose not to live in guilt. He found forgiveness through simple repentance and then he kept on moving forward.

He proclaimed, *"There is therefore now no condemnation to those who are in Christ Jesus, who do not walk according to the flesh, but according to the Spirit"* (Rom. 8:1).

We need to say the same thing to ourselves whenever we struggle with weakness and failure. It is critical that we understand this. The enemy accuses us and causes us to look at the part of us that still needs to be healed. The Holy Spirit, on the other hand,

> ***Healing comes as you surrender your will to His.***

causes us to look at the parts of us that do function properly and that are doing exactly what God wants them to do.

When we see our weakness, it should remind us to pray the "skeleton key prayer" to the Father, to repent of our sins, and to surrender our lives to Him afresh. Wholeness comes as we learn to respond to Him in these ways. Healing comes as we surrender our wills to His.

God is actively involved in your life in so many different ways. There is nothing about you that He does not already know. He is not surprised by your failures. He knows your weaknesses, but He still loves you and wants you to get back "on track" again and follow Him.

YES, YES, YES!

As the daily pressures of life press in upon us, it is often difficult to remember that the Lord is a living Being inside of us. We tend to forget too easily that He has a mind of His own, a will of His own, and desires of His own.

He wants so much for us to yield ourselves to Him so He can live His life through us. He is not interested in our "looking spiritual," whatever that means. Nor is He interested in having us act spiritual.

Our God wants our yes to be yes. He doesn't want us to pretend that He is inside of us. He doesn't want us to be religious either. He wants us to give up all that fleshy stuff and give our lives to Him in complete submission to His Lordship.

God wants us to stop *trying* to be Christians. Instead, He wants us to give ourselves to Him, so He can do in us whatever He wants to do.

> *Relax and let Him do His work in you and through you.*

The problem in all this, however, is that we're used to doing things in certain ways that need changing. We often have habits of thought, religion, practice, and feeling that are opposed to God and His ways.

He wants you to be willing to change. As you learn to look at Him as He truly is, everything will begin to change. Of course, I am assuming that you are willing to allow Him to change you! My guess is that since you have come this far in this book, your heart is open and soft to Him, and your greatest desire is to simply relax and let Him do His work in you and through you.

God is immeasurably great. The psalmist said, *"Great is the Lord, and greatly to be praised"* (Ps. 48:1).

He is greater than our habit patterns, greater than our denominations, greater than our philosophies, greater than our education, and greater than our experience. He is greater than our lifestyle as well. If we allow Him to do so, He will show us how great He is, and He will give us opportunities that we cannot possibly imagine.

So, ask God to give you the courage to say no to your own ways, doctrines, limitations, and fears. He will help you say no to the ways of this world and the things of the past, and He will make all things new in your life.

To let your yes be yes, then, is to let your life be conformed to His will. This is what Paul is saying in his letter to the Romans:

> *And do not be conformed to this world, but be transformed by the renewing of your mind, that you may prove what is that good and acceptable and perfect will of God* (Romans 12:2).

THE WRITTEN WORD OR THE LIVING WORD?

There is a big difference between the written Word and the living Word. We can manipulate the written Word to fit into our own plans and desires. Likewise, we can interpret the written Word in a variety of ways.

Some people, for example, interpret some verses from the Bible as meaning that women should never talk in church, wear makeup or jewelry, or ever wear slacks. Other people interpret other verses as meaning that one should not go to a movie, dance, watch television, or have instrumental music in services.

I think you get the idea. We need the living Word of God—the Lord Jesus Christ—to guide us in understanding His written Word. We need to hear Him speak to our hearts. We need to dwell in His Manifest Presence. The living Word cannot be manipulated. For the Lord Himself acts according to the counsel of His own will, which the written Word reflects. When the living Word acts in a way that is contrary to what we believe the written Word says, we must understand that the living Word is not beholden to our doctrines, He is only beholden to Himself. In the Most Holy Place, His Manifest Presence, He cannot be manipulated, for this is the realm of "all God." Here, we see Him as He is and we are instructed in the ways of the living Word Himself.

Jesus said, *"But the Helper, the Holy Spirit, whom the Father will send in My name, He will teach you all things, and bring to your remembrance all things that I said to you"* (John 14:26). Let the Holy Spirit teach you and guide you into all truth.

One time not long ago I was scheduled to go to London. It was during a period of great personal turmoil, so I ended up not being able to go. However, I sent a friend in my place who also happened to be named Don. Since all this came about at the last minute, communication between my office and London broke down.

My secretary had given my description to the person who was going to meet me at the Heathrow airport. She told him that I was a big guy with a beard and a ponytail and that I wore glasses. Perhaps she also said I looked a little weird!

Certainly, with that description in his mind, I should have been easy to spot. However, the person who went to London was another Don, but he was quite the opposite of me! He was a thin man with short hair, no beard, no ponytail, and no glasses. The one and only obvious similarity between us was our name!

He got off the plane, recovered his luggage, and began looking for the one who was supposed to take him to the hotel. Almost everyone else had gone before he noticed a man who appeared to be waiting for someone. Don took note of the man's puzzled facial expression and how he scratched his head as he was reading the scrap of paper he clutched tightly in his hand.

My friend walked up to the Englishman and said, "Excuse me, are you waiting for somebody from Destiny Image by any chance?"

"Yes, I am."

"Well, I'm the one you're waiting for."

"What? It can't be true. This note says you're a big man with a ponytail and a beard and glasses! You cannot possibly be the one I am looking for!"

Eventually they reached an understanding and Don was able to go with him, but the interesting thing is that the Englishman was bound to the written word instead of believing what his eyes were showing him and his ears were telling him. He initially chose to say "yes" to the written word and "no" to the living word. Only after much conversation was he able to believe the living reality rather than what was written on the paper.

Many Christians are the same way. Even if living proof seemingly contradicts the written Word (or their interpretation of that Word), they become resistant. Many times they will even grow adamant, refusing to change.

Please don't get me wrong. I believe in the Bible. In fact, I love the written Word of God. I have eight different versions of the Scriptures, and I read and study them daily. I believe the Word of God, and I believe that God has never violated His Word.

He is always true to His Word, and He cannot lie. He never goes against His Word. However, every day He will violate what *my* personal interpretation is when it does not accurately represent the reality of the living Word! God is not bound to act according to what I believe about Him. Rather, we are bound to believe Him as He demonstrates Himself to us.

I want to experience the living Word. My fellowship is never with the letter of the Word, because I know that the letter kills. This is not heresy. My relationship is not with a book; it is with Jesus Christ, who is revealed in the Book. The living Spirit of the Word imparts life to me. (See Second Corinthians 3:6.)

EYES HAVE NOT SEEN

The apostle Paul quoted the prophet Isaiah, who wrote, *"Eye has not seen, nor ear heard, nor have entered into the heart of man the things which God has prepared for those who love Him"* (1 Cor. 2:9).

He then went on to explain, *"But God has revealed them to us through His Spirit. For the Spirit searches all things, yes, the deep things of God"* (1 Cor. 2:10).

This is a beautiful description of the difference between adhering to the written Word and responding to the living Word. Believing that God has prepared each for me makes me wake up every day with a renewed sense of wonder and anticipation—because I realize that each new day is an opportunity to experience the living Presence of Jesus, as He leads me step by step and reveals Himself and His ways to me.

The Holy Spirit reveals the deep things of God to us, and I want to hear His voice speaking to me and showing me those wonderful, deep things. I am not happy with anything less than the Manifest Presence of God.

> *Your Lord has a lot to say to you.*

When I stand behind a pulpit, I cannot just preach a sermon—a written, well-polished treatise that I've prepared for the people. I just can't do it that way anymore. If I don't know that the living Presence of Almighty God is speaking through me, I don't have anything to say to the people. To speak to folks without the knowledge that God has something to say to them through me, at that moment, is grossly unfair to the people and leaves them and me unfulfilled, not to mention all the wasted time involved!

Our Lord has a lot to say to us. But He will mostly speak to us Spirit to spirit. He will give us ample opportunity to agree with Him and His plan, if we will get out of the way. This is how we can hear His voice.

He has more for us than we can possibly imagine, so when He speaks, it will most often be outside of our comfort zone as well as beyond what our religious instruction permits. We need to quiet our hearts and listen to Him, the One who is waiting to lead us into the most wondrous adventures of our lives.

When you hear Him, your response should naturally be, "Yes, Lord!" This allows Heaven to open its doors and manipulate circumstances so as to do what He is showing you to do. If He can part the Red Sea, He can make His own way through the systems and struggles of the world in order to accomplish the dream He has most certainly dreamed for you!

He who calls you is faithful, who also will do it (1 Thessalonians 5:24).

About Don Nori, Sr.

Don Nori, Sr. has worked in the publishing industry and ministered internationally for more than 25 years, working with people of all races and nationalities. Don and his wife, Cathy, live at the foot of the Appalachian Mountains in south central Pennsylvania where they raised their five sons and now enjoy their daughters-in-law and their grandchildren.

Chapter 2

SPIRIT-EMPOWERED PRAYER STORM

by James Goll

"I have heard you," replied Jeremiah the prophet. "I will certainly pray to the Lord your God as you have requested; I will tell you everything the Lord says and will keep nothing back from you" (Jeremiah 42:4 NIV).

For this chapter, I have chosen to use the term, *Spirit-empowered prayer*, although I have presented similar biblical overviews of prayer under different headings such as *prophetic intercession* or *revelatory prayer*. It seems that the idea of *Spirit-empowered prayer* is easier to grasp than some of the other terms that I and others have often used. What do I mean by the term? It's straightforward enough; I'm talking about prayer that is directed and led by the Holy Spirit.

This kind of prayer is like being in a great waltz in which you let the Holy Spirit take the lead. He not only leads you, but He also propels you. He not only nudges you this way and that, but He sometimes keeps you dancing all night! Spirit-empowered prayer is like getting a booster to your prayer rocket. Just like He did on the day of Pentecost in the Book of Acts (see Acts 2), the Holy Spirit comes upon you and rises up within you. He gives you a burst of power, energy, and insight that you did not possess previously.

> *The Holy Spirit gives you a refreshing burst of power, energy, and insight.*

Paul wrote these words to the church in Rome: *"All who are being led by the Spirit of God, these are the sons of God"* (Rom. 8:14 NASB). As God's children, naturally we want to be led by Him. We want to keep up with Him. We want to walk in His footsteps. It doesn't take us very long before we realize that we cannot accomplish this without the power of the Holy Spirit. In our humanity, we do not come equipped with the kind of power—the impetus, the insight, the influence—that is required to accomplish God's work. We need to be filled with divine power.

Prophetic intercession is the ability to receive an immediate prayer request from God and to pray about it in a divinely anointed utterance. *Prophetic prayer* is waiting before God in order to "hear" or receive God's burden (which means God's concern, warning, conditions, vision, promise, or word) and then responding back to the Lord and to the people, with appropriate actions. The types of prayer, whatever you want to call them (prophetic intercession, prophetic prayer, revelatory prayer), and the appropriate actions (responses and "techniques" of prayer) are all included under Spirit-empowered prayer.

THE POWER OF PROPHETIC INTERCESSION

In my book, *The Prophetic Intercessor,* I developed the biblical basis for prophetic intercession with thorough teaching and numerous examples from Church history and my own life's journey. But for this chapter, let me simply give you an overview of this subject that is so dear to my heart.

In the Scripture I quoted at the beginning of this chapter, Jeremiah the prophet agreed to pray on behalf of the people, and he agreed to listen to God for them. This is what prophets do—they can "hear" God (whether or not they hear an audible voice), and they are able to tell people what God has said. In this instance, Jeremiah was combining his prophetic role with the priestly role of intercession.

In prophetic intercession, the roles of priest and prophet are brought together. Not all prophets are intercessors, and not all priests are prophets. But when these two come together, it can be powerful! In authentic prophetic intercession, the graces and burdens of the prophet and the priest are united. The priest pleads the needs of the people to the Lord. The prophet pleads the interests of God before the people. The prophetic intercessor does both.

PROPHETIC INTERCESSION PLEADS THE PROMISES

As an intercessor rises in worship, he or she becomes securely seated with Christ Jesus in the heavenly places. As a result, the intercessor receives a revelation of His heart. With that revelation, the intercessor is able to pray *with* God instead of merely *to* Him from his or her own limited perspective and passion. The intercessor becomes prophetic. The words of intercession become reiterations of God's Word. They match up with the will of God. The prophetic intercessor pleads the promises of God.

This makes an amazing difference in the effectiveness of prayer. When God enables you to pray like this, your prayers can be based not only on the covenant promises of God that He has made to His people and that are recorded in the Bible, but also on the rest of the unfulfilled promises that He has made to His people throughout history.

You are like John the Beloved, leaning your head upon the chest of the Messiah. You are hearing the very heartbeat of Heaven, and that heartbeat begins to resonate within you. Your words of prayer arise from your heart, which is filled with His Spirit, and that means that they are guaranteed to be in agreement with God—which makes them highly effective.

The words of this kind of revelatory prayer pave the way for the realization of as-yet-unfulfilled prophetic promises. In this kind of prophetic intercession, the Spirit of God pleads through you as a believer. Your prayer "targets" are painted with greater accuracy. Not only does the Spirit urge you to pray prayers that have been prayed for centuries ("Come, Lord Jesus"), but He also enables you, as a Spirit-filled intercessor, to "pick up on" immediate prayer requests that are on the heart of God ("Lord, anoint the preaching of Your Word this evening"). The Holy Spirit nudges you to pray for particular things in particular ways so that He can intervene. You are given revelation for situations about which you have very little knowledge in the natural. Whether your prayer requests are small or large, you know you can be confident that they will be bringing forth His will on the earth as it is willed in Heaven.

THE ANNA COMPANY

God is looking for a particular kind of people. He is looking for Holy Ghost *pushers*. He's looking for people who He can put on assignment, people who will press and push in their praying until something happens. He wants these people to join hands and take their places as watchmen on the wall for His sake, for the sake of His coming Kingdom. He is looking for Annas and Simeons who will pray relentlessly:

> *Now there was a man in Jerusalem called Simeon, who was righteous and devout. He was waiting for the consolation of Israel, and the Holy Spirit was upon him. It had been revealed to him by the Holy Spirit that he would not die before he had seen the Lord's Christ* (Luke 2:25-26 NIV).

> *And there was a prophetess, Anna the daughter of Phanuel, of the tribe of Asher She was advanced in years and had lived with her husband seven years after her marriage, and then as a widow to the age of eighty-four. She never left the temple, serving night and day with fastings and prayers. At that very moment she came up and began giving thanks to God, and continued to speak of Him to all those who were looking for the redemption of Jerusalem* (Luke 2:36-38 NASB).

Anna's assignment was prayer, specifically prayer that would prepare the way for the coming of the Messiah. Her story helps us understand our own prayer assignments. She stayed there in the temple, fasting and praying, day after day, week after week, year after year. She worshiped and prayed through the promises of God. God had promised to send a Savior. She was waiting for Him, not passively or with resignation, but actively, with prayer.

I believe that, just as God had Anna and Simeon before the first coming of Jesus, so it will be before His Second Coming. I believe that there will be consecrated, gifted, prophetic intercessors who will lay hold of the purposes of God. May it happen in this generation!

> *Are you waiting for Him, not passively, but actively, with prayer?*

The Lord wants to raise up an Anna company in our day, intercessors who will pave the way for the second coming of the Lord. He is looking for new recruits; the Holy Spirit is sending out invitations. Have you responded yet?

Now when I say "Anna company," I don't mean that this assignment is for women only. It's true that many of the greatest intercessors of our time have been women. They have a natural sensitivity of spirit and a passion for the things of God. They are ready to yield their hearts to Him to plead his cause. But the Anna company is made up of both men and women, young as well as old. The only qualification that you need, in order to belong, is an ever-growing conviction of the end-time purposes of God and a desire to pray through God's promises until you see them fulfilled.

The members of the Anna company know how the burden of prophetic intercession begins as a small flame and soon consumes everything around it as revelation increases. They know how the burden grows throughout its "gestation period," and they learn how to travail and how to push in prayer in order to bring God's purposes to birth. All prophetic intercession carries with it the struggle of birth. The hearts of prophetic intercessors becomes wombs in which God's prophetic purposes can grow until it's time for them to come forth. Arise, people of God, and put off your slumber! Let us become steadfast and single-minded, like Anna, more than 2,000 years ago. When we see Him, let us cry out, "Behold the Christ!"

PROPHETIC INTERCESSION = CONSPIRING

The word *conspire* means "to breathe together." When God created man from the dust of the earth, He breathed into his nostrils the breath of life, and man became a living being (see Gen. 2:7). This Hebrew word that we translate "breathed" can mean breathing violently, such as when the violent, rushing wind filled the upper room on the day of Pentecost.[1]

The prophetic intercessor *conspires* with God that His glory will be seen, felt, and known in the earth. Prophetic intercession is our conspiring (breathing together) with God, breathing violently into situations through prayer in order to bring forth life. Here's an example from my own life.

Some years back, I was in Germany. In the middle of the night, I took a train from Heidelberg to Rosenheim, which is in the part of southern Germany that is known as Bavaria. It was a six-hour trip. All night long, as I attempted to rest on the train, I kept hearing the gentle, consistent voice of the Holy Spirit. After a while, it was as if I were breathing these words with Him. The same phrase rumbled over and over within my mind and heart as the train rumbled its way across Germany: "Where are my Daniels? Where are my Esthers? Where are my Deborahs? Where are my Josephs?" I heard it over and over. "Where are my Daniels? Where are my Esthers? Where are my Deborahs? Where are my Josephs?"

I knew He was talking to me as an individual intercessor, but I also felt He was imparting to me a burden to raise up a band of people who would volunteer themselves for the task of prayer. It was as if the Spirit and I were *con-spiring*, breathing together, for the purpose of bringing life into something that was in the heart of God. Where *are* His Daniels, Esthers, Deborahs, and Josephs? Are you one of them? Have you been positioned *"for such a time as this"*? (See Esther 4:14.) Have you been brought forth for this prophetic intercessory task? Will you be one of the answers to His persistent plea?

Many years ago, I saw a vision of "velvet warriors" moving forward on their knees. It was the army of the Lord, but they were coming so much more slowly than I would have anticipated. When I saw them come to the top of a hill, I could see why—they were marching on their knees. Then the Spirit described them to me as velvet warriors. This indicated that they were part of an arising generation that knew that its strength was on bended knee.

> *Will you be one of the answers to His persistent plea?*

That army is still assembling, and many vacancies still exist in it; you can still sign up. It's not too late to answer the call. You can volunteer for on-the-job training and be commissioned as one of God's servant warriors. I think I can hear drumbeats in the background. I think I can hear another sound calling forth watchmen to mount their walls. Who will answer these calls? Who will blend their heartbeat and their heart's cry with His?

FORMS OF SPIRIT-EMPOWERED PRAYER

Spirit-empowered prayer can take many forms, as the Spirit blows wherever He wishes. But two forms of Spirit-inspired prayer, which are completely biblical and completely under the oversight of the Holy Spirit, are praying in the Spirit through the gift of tongues and praying in the Spirit through intense, fervent prayer (prayer that is so intense it is like the "travail" of natural childbirth). Tongues and travail. I want to spend the rest of the chapter on these two forms of prayer.

The Gift of Tongues

The gift of tongues—what a wonderful dimension of prayer! I love to pray in tongues. I probably pray in this way more than I do in any other way. Of course, I pray in English all the time. I read the Word of God, and then I pray it. But one of the keys that opens revelation for me is praying in tongues, first in a devotional way and then, as the Spirit arises within me, in the intercessory dimension of the gift. I'm not saying that it's the only way to pray, because it's not; it's just a way. There are many forms of Spirit-led, Spirit-empowered prayer. But praying with the gift of tongues is one of the primary ones.

When you pray in the Spirit, your spirit is communicating directly with God. It's a straight shot. You can pray in your prayer language as much as you want to, using it to raise yourself up to new levels in praise, worship, and intercession. The Word tells us: *"For anyone who speaks in a tongue does not speak to men but to God. Indeed, no one understands him; he utters mysteries with his spirit"* (1 Cor. 14:2 NIV).

When you pray privately in this way, whether quietly or loudly, sitting at your desk, standing at the kitchen sink, or driving your car, you are edifying and building yourself up in the Lord, uttering far more expressive praises to Him than you could think up on your own.

But you can also use this spiritual gift to intercede. You can bring a concern, care, or burden before the Lord and yield it to Him with words in your prayer language. In this way, the Holy Spirit intercedes through your spirit:

> *The Spirit helps us in our weakness. We do not know what we ought to pray for, but the Spirit Himself*

intercedes for us with groans that words cannot express. And He who searches our hearts knows the mind of the Spirit, because the Spirit intercedes for the saints in accordance with God's will (Romans 8:26-28 NIV).

For if I pray in an [unknown] tongue, my spirit [by the Holy Spirit within me] prays, but my mind is unproductive [it bears no fruit and helps nobody] (1 Corinthians 14:14 AMP).

Since none of us always knows how or what to pray in a given situation, bringing your prayer before the Lord by praying in the Spirit enables the Holy Spirit, your Helper, to pray within the Lord's will. Using a prayer language is a way of being dependent upon God, because you cannot duplicate it or invent it on your own. Sometimes people might act proud of it, as in "I have something better than you do," but needless to say, all that reveals is a character weakness in the speaker, not a flaw in the gift itself.

Years ago, when I did not yet exercise the gift of tongues, I thought I didn't need it. I said, "God gives that to those who need it, and I don't need it." As the next few months went by, the Lord convinced me that the first part of my statement was totally correct. God does give the gift to those who need it. But the second part of my statement was not correct, because I did need it! I had come up against some circumstances in my life that I could not solve. I wasn't trained enough. I wasn't knowledgeable enough. I wasn't experienced enough. I didn't seem to have enough prayer power on my own, so I yielded to the Holy Spirit. I now had a new revelation: God gives the gift to those who need it. And, guess what, that includes me. That was humbling.

Even though praying in the Spirit sounds nonsensical to your ear (because you really don't know what you're saying), your prayer language has definite meaning. It doesn't matter whether or not you understand it, because God does, and He is the One you are praying to. He who inspired it also comprehends it. First Corinthians 14:10 explains that *"undoubtedly there are all sorts of languages in the world, yet none of them is without meaning"* (NIV).

Use this gift often, because it will edify your spirit. You will be built up and strengthened, encouraged and reinvigorated for your intercessory warfare task. We read again in the 14th chapter of First Corinthians: *"One who speaks in a tongue edifies himself"* (1 Cor. 14:4a NASB). In the Book of Jude, we read, *"But you, dear friends, build yourselves up in your most holy faith and pray in the Holy Spirit"* (Jude 20 NIV). So if you want to be in the Spirit and stay in the Spirit—pray in the Spirit!

> *You will be built up and strengthened, encouraged and reinvigorated for your intercessory warfare task.*

Praying in the Spirit has the full authority of Heaven behind it! There is no way you could know in the natural when satan and his demonic forces are about to launch an attack, but the Holy Spirit will prompt you at the strategic, opportune time and will keep you on the alert. And because you know that *"the effective prayer of a righteous man can accomplish much"* (James 5:16b NASB), you can be sure that you will prevail. You just prayed prayers that were inspired by the Spirit. And who is more righteous than the Holy Spirit?

You can pray both ways, in the Spirit and with your mind. That's what Paul did: *"...I will pray with the spirit and I will pray with the mind also; I will sing with the spirit and I will sing with the mind also"* (1 Cor. 14:15 NASB). Like Paul, you can pray in the Spirit to regain territory from the demonic kingdom, and you can express your prayers with unfailing faith and unwavering joy, praise, and worship. This prayer and praise weapon is powerful, and it's always on target. Praying in the Spirit is God's anti-ballistic missile, and it hits the mark every time!

Paul further instructed us about the gift of tongues:

> *Now concerning spiritual gifts, brethren, I would not have you ignorant.... Now there are diversities of gifts, but the same Spirit. And there are differences of administrations, but the same Lord. And there are diversities of operations, but it is the same God which worketh all in all. But the manifestation of the Spirit is given to every man to profit withal.... Now ye are the body of Christ, and members in particular. And God hath set some in the church, first apostles, secondarily prophets, thirdly teachers, after that miracles, then gifts of healings, helps, governments, diversities of tongues* (1 Corinthians 12:1,4-7,27-28 KJV).

He was saying, obviously, that there are different kinds of tongues. They sound different—really different—from each other. In that passage, the word translated "diversities" is *genos* in the Greek, and it refers to a collection of different things that belong to the same group or family, "kin" or "offspring."[2] In other words, diversities of tongues are all heavenly utterances that are as different as the members of a family or group can be, but they related to one another by the same Spirit.

As you know, the Holy Spirit loves diversity. If you have ever traveled widely, you will know what I mean. Not only is God's creation vast and filled with infinite variety, but human cultures and languages are too. I have traveled in well over 40 different nations on all of the continents, and I have heard some very strange dialects. Some languages sound like baby talk or just noise to my ear. But they are all languages, and they all have meaning. So if you hear other people speaking in prayer languages that don't sound very sophisticated to you—that's OK. Even in one person's range of experience with this gift, we see diversity.

This may be a bit of a review, but here are some diverse applications from the Bible for the gift of tongues:

- Tongues at the filling of the Holy Spirit (See Acts 2:1-4; 10:44-46; Mark 16:17.)

- Tongues for interpretation (See 1 Corinthians 12:7-10; Isaiah 28:11.)

- Tongues of edification (See Jude 20; 1 Corinthians 14:4.)

- Tongues as a sign to the unbeliever (See 1 Corinthians 14:22.)

- Tongues of intercession (See Romans 8:26. The word *groanings* in this verse can be translated as "inarticulate speech," and it refers to speech that does not originate in the intellect or with the understanding, speech that is not related to race or nationality. Inarticulate speech includes, but is not limited to, "other tongues.")[3]

- Tongues of warfare (Sometimes the Holy Spirit goes on the offensive. He battles through us. Sometimes He couples together the gift of tongues with the gift of faith or the gift of discerning of spirits. You will feel a rising up inside and a push or an urge to launch out against demonic forces. You attack the powers of darkness, taking authority over satan and rejecting his plans, and you do it by the power of the Holy

Spirit who dwells within you. This is your tongue of intercession engaged in warfare, bringing deliverance, healing, and liberty.)

The Prayer of Groaning and Travail

Let's examine more in depth the Scripture I cited above under "tongues of intercession." Before long, most committed intercessors have the experience described in Romans 8:26-27, the experience of the Holy Spirit groaning and wrestling through their prayers. Here are two translations of these two verses:

> *In the same way the Spirit also helps our weakness; for we do not know how to pray as we should, but the Spirit Himself intercedes for us with groanings too deep for words; and He who searches the hearts knows what the mind of the Spirit is, because He intercedes for the saints according to the will of God* (Romans 8:26-27 NASB).

> *So too the [Holy] Spirit comes to our aid and bears us up in our weakness; for we do not know what prayer to offer nor how to offer it worthily as we ought, but the Spirit Himself goes to meet our supplication and pleads in our behalf with unspeakable yearnings and groanings too deep for utterance. And He Who searches the hearts of men knows what is in the mind of the [Holy] Spirit [what His intent is], because the Spirit intercedes and pleads [before God] in behalf of the saints according to and in harmony with God's will* (Romans 8:26-27 AMP).

Many times we call this kind of praying "travail," because it is so much like natural childbirth. It is the will of God to give birth to His purposes, but that process of birthing is not instantaneous or painless. It can be quite a struggle. Words alone can't accomplish it. The Holy Spirit in us moves beyond words to sighs, groans, and inarticulate longings. We move with our prayers. We may stand up and reach up to God, then pace, then fall to the floor, even writhing as we yearn for the relief of the longed-for "birth." It's work. It's very much like labor, purposeful and intense. In the heat of the effort, we no longer worry about maintaining our dignity.

This kind of praying is fervent. It is hot. (The word *fervent* comes from the Latin word for "to boil; hot.")[4] In this kind of intercession, we see God's intense desire to create an opening through which He can bring new life, change, growth, or fruit. Elijah modeled it for us:

> *Elijah was a man with a nature like ours, and he prayed earnestly that it would not rain, and it did not rain on the earth for three years and six months. Then he prayed again, and the sky poured rain and the earth produced its fruit* (James 5:17-18 NASB).

Prayer that involves groaning and panting under the power of the Holy Spirit, like a woman in childbirth, can also be compared to the heat of a conflict on a battlefield. Look at two more verses, which happen to combine the two images:

> *The Lord will go forth like a mighty man, He will rouse up His zealous indignation and vengeance like a warrior; He will cry, yes, He will shout aloud, He will do mightily against His enemies. [Thus says the Lord] I have for a long time held My peace, I have been still and restrained Myself. Now I will cry out like a woman in travail, I will gasp and pant together* (Isaiah 42:13-14 AMP).

Jesus is our example in fervent prayer. Often He was *not* hushed and quiet when He prayed. He was stirred to the depths of His being, to the point that He could not suppress His explosive sighs. (Remember the story of Lazarus' death and resurrection in John 11:33-44.) The writer of Hebrews tells us that when Jesus walked the earth as the Son of Man, one way He showed His humanity was by the way He prayed: *"In the days of His flesh [Jesus] offered up definite, special petitions...and supplications with strong crying and tears"* (Heb. 5:7a AMP).

"Strong crying and tears," especially the Greek term for it, gives the idea that He cried out loudly in prayer, even shouting and screaming.[5] It was the sound of the battlefield, a struggle of life and death. In no way was it timid or restrained.

The prayer of groaning brings deliverance from within and pushes back the pressures of darkness from without. Walls of resistance toward God are within each of us. We hardly see them, and we definitely cannot deliver ourselves from them, but this kind of prayer is higher than our understanding. It is larger than our limited comprehension, because it bypasses our minds and allows the Holy Spirit to move us into the freedom that God desires.

The prayer of groaning originates deep within our spirits. It is deep calling unto deep. It brings release from the grave clothes of dead works, stripping us so that we might be re-clothed by the Spirit of God. We long for even a foretaste of things to come, and we want to be prepared: *"For indeed in this house we groan, longing to be clothed with our dwelling from heaven"* (2 Cor. 5:2 NASB).

Travailing prayer comes before the promise is born, but not before the promise is conceived. Intimacy with God allows the "conception," as the promise is revealed and received into our spirits. But travail is how the birth is achieved. It opens up the way, removes the hindrances and constraints, and creates a broad "highway" for God's promise to be shown forth into the light of day (see Isa. 40:3).

When Elijah prayed, he gave it all he had (see James 5:17). We have a description of his posture—he prayed with his face between his knees, crouched to the earth (see 1 Kings 18:42). That is a travailing posture. It's not the only kind of prayer; it's just one kind. But it's good to be aware of it in case the Holy Spirit brings you into the experience or you are in a place (hopefully a behind-the-scenes place) with other intercessors where it happens.

A good example of this kind of praying happened to me—along with a team of men—in 1986 in Haiti. I had gone there many times, but this time I was there with my friend, Mahesh Chavda, doing intercession before, during, and after his times of preaching. Many miracles had occurred, and many people had come to Jesus. Well, one time, in the middle of the night, I went with a small team up to an outlook over Port-au-Prince, the capital city. We felt that the Holy Spirit wanted us to go there. This was back when Jean-Claude "Baby Doc" Duvalier was dictator of the country, and he was as ruthless and decadent as his father ("Papa Doc") had been. The country had suffered for so long; it had become the poorest nation in the western hemisphere.

We got up in the middle of the night and went up to the overlook, burdened for the nation of Haiti. As a team, we had been praying and fasting. There in the darkness, overlooking the lights of the city, travailing prayer came upon us like a blanket, in a split second, as if the team members were one man. Instantly, we were praying in agreement in a

> *Our prayers went beyond the articulation of natural speech.*

prayer dimension that went beyond our understanding and previous experience. Our prayers went beyond the articulation of natural speech. We were like women in travail.

47

Being men, none of us had ever had children, so you could argue that I don't know what I'm talking about. But I had been with my wife four times in the birthing room, so I think I do know, at least partially, what it's like. One thing I know about it is that, once you're underway, you can't back up. You can't just put travail on "pause," even if you want to, anymore than you can stop labor and delivery from happening. You're committed to it, and you go with it, even if you don't look very calm, cool, and collected while it's happening.

We travailed until the Spirit lifted, and then we went back to where we had been staying. The next day, we heard the news: Baby Doc had fled the country. He was gone, headed for exile in France. His dictatorship had ended. This opened a season of mercy for the Haitians. It didn't solve every problem, but they did have the first democratic election in their history, and the rule of the Duvalier family had ended.

BE TENACIOUS

I want to mention one more thing. Travail takes time. You have to be tenacious. You will go through stretches when you are not crying out. In fact, nothing seems to be happening. It's more like being a watchman on a wall when nothing is happening. But you stay there. You don't abandon your post. You keep alert. You don't flag in your attention. You persevere. You need to be ready if the Holy Spirit is ready.

The psalmist wrote, *"I pursued my enemies and overtook them, and I did not turn back until they were consumed"* (Ps. 18:37 NASB). When did he quit? When the battle was over. He didn't quit in the middle, and he didn't take a break.

That's what Spirit-empowered prayer is like. The Holy Spirit's energy does not flag. When you're praying in the power of the Spirit, you will not give up. You will be able to go far beyond your normal ability to pray, even if you possess a lot of natural energy and zeal. You are breathing together, "con-spiring." As you do it, you get better at it. You keep pursuing your enemy until you over take him, and you keep laboring until you have a breakthrough.

When you undertake Spirit-empowered prayer, you operate with a watchman's anointing. You watch to see things in the Spirit. What is the enemy up to? What does God want to do about it? You take the keys of the Kingdom in your hand, and you bind up the darkness. You welcome the Spirit of the Lord's presence. You are vigilant and determined. You communicate with your fellow watchers. Together, you maintain the watch.

> *Father, I want to make a difference! I want to be one of the members of your spiritual armed forces, and I want to help to bring in Your Kingdom by force (see Matt. 11:12). Anoint me with Spirit-empowered prayer power that goes beyond my natural mind. Take me further in prayer than I have ever been before, for Your Kingdom's sake. I want to storm against the foe in prayer. Your Kingdom come, Your will be done, on earth as it is in Heaven. In Jesus' name, amen.*

About Dr. James W. Goll

Dr. James W. Goll is the President of Encounters Network, Director of Prayer Storm, and coordinates Encounters Alliance, a coalition of leaders. He is the Founder of the God Encounters Training E-School of the Heart and has shared Jesus in more than 40 nations worldwide. Teaching and imparting the power of intercession and prophetic ministry, exalting Christ Jesus and living a life filled with the Holy Spirit is His passion.

Endnotes

1. *Merriam-Webster's Collegiate Dictionary*, 11th ed., s.v. "Conspire"; from Latin "conspirare." "Breathed" or "Naphach"; http://www.studylight.org/lex/heb/view.cgi?number=05301.

2. "Genos"; see http://www.studylight.org/lex/grk/view.cgi?number =1085.

3. "Groanings"; http://www.studylight.org/lex/grk/view.cgi?number =4726.

4. *Merriam-Webster's Collegiate Dictionary*, 11th ed., s.v. "Fervent."

5. "ischuros/forcible," http://www.studylight.org/lex/grk/view .cgi?number=2478; "krauge/crying," http://www.studylight .org/lex/grk/view.cgi?number=2906; "dakru/tears," http://www .studylight .org/lex/grk/view.cgi?number=1144.

Chapter 3

MYSTICS, MYSTICAL EXPERIENCES, AND CONTEMPLATIVE PRAYER

by Beni Johnson

Deep calls unto deep at the noise of Your waterfalls; all Your waves and billows have gone over me (Psalm 42:7).

This chapter is dedicated to the mystics, the contemplatives, those now and those who have gone on before us, those who have lived in deep communion with the Three-ness, the Trinity. The mystics call their communion, "ecstasies." As you read this chapter, my hope and prayer is that you will experience the realms of ecstasy, the realms where you are called to the deep places of God, and that His water will flow over you.

I've found myself being drawn to learning as much as I can about the mystics. To me, "mystics" are the people who have laid down their entire lives to seek after one thing, the very heart of God. One of the things that make "mystics" different from other people is that they have only one desire, to know God in His fullness.

Mystics are people who live in right relationship with God and who have truly surrendered themselves to knowing Him more, no matter what the cost. Mystics do not seek after fame, glory, or worldly desires, but they have chosen instead to lay their entire lives down so that they can hear the heartbeat of Heaven. Mystics are people who have a continual awareness of God.

> *Mystics see beyond this reality and into the spirit realm.*

Mystics are not satisfied with what is in front of them. They want to see more. Mystics see beyond this reality and into the spirit realm.

To them, God is more real than life. God is their life. Mystics see how the spirit realm connects with the worldly realms. In other words, they see how and where Heaven is invading earth. They take all of those connections, and they put them together and make sense of it all. Mystics are able to see into the spiritual realm and use it to help define what is going on in the earthly realm. In this sense, they help to bring Heaven to earth.

To the mystic, the spirit realm is a safe place. To them, the spiritual realm can often seem more real than the earthly realm. In fact, a mystic thrives on experiencing that heavenly realm.

There are many different types of mystics. One of those types is what some call a *cave dweller.* The Desert Fathers who lived as hermits are often referred to as cave dwellers. A cave dweller likes to be alone with God and would spend all of his time alone with God if he could. Once, when I was traveling, I met a young man who I instantly knew was a cave dweller. I asked him, and he agreed that he was a cave dweller. I can't really explain how I knew that he was a cave dweller, but I could just tell. I could see it in his eyes and on his face and all around him in the spiritual realm. I could tell that he was one who preferred to spend his time alone with God. I could tell that he was a friend of God.

Another type of mystic is a seer. A seer is able to *see* into the spiritual realm and discern the times and seasons that we are living in. One example of that type of mystic is Bob Jones. Bob Jones is a seer prophet.

CONNECTION WITH GOD

I know when I am really in that place where I feel completely connected to God because I have an instant peace. When I am in that place, it feels as though everything makes sense and becomes "centered" in an instant. In that place, I experience a peace and warmth that could be described as nothing but truly divine. It is almost saying "aahhh" in my spirit, soul, and body. There is nothing on earth that is like that feeling. It is pure ecstasy.

I have found that, because I have spent time in the presence of God and have learned how to access His presence, it has become easier for me to connect with God. And because I have developed that connection, when I turn my attention to God, I can immediately begin to feel His presence.

Because I know what it feels like to be connected with God, I have become much more aware of how it feels when I have lost that connection. I have learned that, when I am not walking in that connecting place with God where I feel His presence, I begin to feel insecure. The best way that I can describe this feeling is that, all of a sudden, everything begins to feel out of sorts, and I have to reconnect with the heart of God and His presence to make everything feel like it has fallen back into its right place again, and once things fall back into place, they become "rightly fitted."

Another way that I can tell if I'm not at that connecting place with God is that I begin to let outside influences affect my emotions, my spirit man, and my decisions because I am not connected to what is truly real. *"While we do not look at the things which are seen, but at the things which are not seen, for the things which are seen are temporary, but the things which are not seen are eternal"* (2 Cor. 4:18).

When we connect with God, we make ourselves aware that He is right there all the time. And I have learned that I can experience that reality of the presence of God no matter where I am or what I am doing. It is an awareness that He is right there when I am in my car, while I am taking a walk, or playing with my grandchildren. And because I have spent time with God, focusing on His presence, I have found that I now have access to an instant connection.

Mystics—Super and Natural

To me, the mystics are just normal people. They are normal people consumed by the presence of God. They are normal people who enjoy being with God and who know how to move in and out of the secret place.

I used to think of mystics as people who just stayed secluded with God and hid themselves away from other people and from the world. But many of the mystics did not stay secluded. In fact, a lot of them lived in the world and touched the world. Saints Patrick and Columba are examples of two mystics who chose to impact the world around them with the Kingdom of God.

These two men were great evangelists who moved in signs and wonders. Although they lived for the heartbeat of Heaven, they also chose to bring the Kingdom of Heaven to the earth. They knew how to touch the Father's heart, yet they moved among the people and ministered. And a long time ago, I decided that, if they can do both, I can do both.

A lot of times, when people think of mystics, they think of secluded people who run away from everything, but that is not always the case. Some of the people whom I would describe as modern-day mystics live extremely normal lives. Some of the most mystical people I know today are able to function in the world around them, even though they spend much of their time living in the spiritual realm. They get their life and their breath from the secret place. The most important thing to them is seeking the face of God, and they have a desire and a passion to know what God is doing and to hear what He is saying. They are desperate to hear the heartbeat of Heaven. Without that connection with Heaven, they begin to feel unbalanced.

The mystics are no different than you and me. They are everyday people who have chosen to lay their lives down to seek after God. They do not limit God. Mystics seek after God with their whole hearts. They go before God and say, "God, You are all that I desire. No matter what it looks like, or what it costs me, I must have more of You." The heart cry of the mystic is, "Take the world but give me You."

In the Bible, King David was a mystic. David did things way before his time. For example, David opened up worship for everybody. He opened it up for people to worship and be with God in the tabernacle. He made worship available. He said, we can all do this.

A mystical person who is in a right relationship with God and humankind will naturally open the gates for other people to go to the same places in the spiritual realm that he or she has discovered. We see this in Psalm 27:4, when David cries, *"One thing I have desired of the Lord, that will I seek: that I may dwell in the house of the Lord all of the days of my life, to behold the beauty of the Lord and to inquire in His temple."*

There are so many things that we can glean from the life of David. When we read the Bible, we can see that David made a lot of mistakes. But Paul writes, quoting from the Old Testament, in Acts 13:22, about God saying of David, *"I have found David the son of Jesse, a man after My own heart, who will do all My will."* David was a man after the heart of God. He pursued the Lord and His presence and was desperate to intimately know the heart of God. David was just a man. But he had a heart after God. And David's heart after God had that mystical essence to it. We can see that in his writing of the Psalms, in his earnest desire to be one with his Maker and to be known by His God. This is the heart cry of the mystic: to be one with God.

THE ONENESS

When I spend time in the secret place, alone with God, I become so wrapped up in His presence that every other desire loses its importance to me. When I allow His presence to consume me, I surrender myself so completely to His will that my desires begin to line up with His. I become fully engulfed in His presence, lost in a sea of His beauty, and captivated by His love. In that place is the fullness of joy, the fullness of peace, the fullness of love, and the fullness of acceptance. In that place, I become one with Him. And in that place, I have found myself "caught up" in many different types of mystical experiences.

MYSTICAL EXPERIENCES

God wants us to understand His world and His Kingdom. He wants us to know all about Him and to know Him intimately. He wants to tell us His secrets and to share His heart with us. Often, when we experience these things, they come through mystical experiences. Mystical experiences are often difficult for our earthly minds to comprehend. It is as though they come from another world, secrets whispered to us from above.

Several years ago in one of our services, I had an encounter with Heaven that I would describe as a mystical experience. During this experience, the Lord took me into a vision where I walked out onto a beautiful ridge. There was a soft light over the

> ***They didn't know that they needed help.***

ridge. As I walked out onto this ridge, I saw, off to the right overlooking a vast valley, Jesus sitting. I looked into the valley. It went on forever. There seemed to be no end to the valley. In the valley were thousands of people just standing. The best way to describe them was that they looked like dead men walking. They had the form of humans but were empty inside. The funny thing is that they were all holding suitcases. As I looked on, I realized that they were starting to ascend to the top of the ridge one at a time. As the first man came up the ridge, he came and stood right in front of me. The feeling was that they were in desperate need, for they were dead inside. They needed someone to help them. But, at the same time, they didn't know that they needed help.

I looked over at Jesus and didn't understand why He wasn't coming to help. There was no verbal communication between Jesus, but we communicated spirit-to-Spirit, which I think of as Spirit talk. As I looked to Jesus, out from behind Him came flying the Holy Spirit. He was not in human form but in a blue-white energy form. He was this amazing form of energy that flew in every direction. He came right to the dead man and began flying and swirling around him. Jesus communicated to me at that moment that it was my responsibility to help the man. What he had in his suitcase was the key for help. I reached down and opened the suitcase and pulled out clothing. The clothing was spirit clothing. It was destiny, his personal giftings, and who this man really was. I just began dressing him, and the Holy Spirit was equipping him by swirling around him. As I dressed him in who he was called to be, the death left him. He was alive in spirit. That was the end of the vision. The vision filled me with a lot of emotion. The thing that was impressed on me the most was my partnering with the Holy Spirit who is light and energy.

I've thought about that vision many times. I realize now that in the vision Jesus didn't do anything because He already had done it on the cross. The Holy Spirit came because the Holy Spirit was sent to help us. I learned in that vision that the Holy Spirit is wild and full of heavenly energy. He never stops. He is always on the move. I'm so thankful for that vision because it gave me more understanding of the Trinity. When God gives us visions and dreams, it is to give us instruction and revelation into His realm. It is to understand that deep realm of the Spirit. *"I will give you the treasures of darkness and hidden riches of secret places that you may know that I, the Lord, who call you by your name, Am the God of Israel"* (Isa. 45:3).

LET THE WALLS COME DOWN

Some people fear the intimate places of the Lord. They are afraid that God is not good and that He won't protect them. They fear the things of God and the spiritual realm. As a result, they put up walls to God because they are afraid. But when we come to a place where we truly believe that God is good, that He is our heavenly Father, we can put those fears aside and dive into new realms of the Spirit and begin to experience the fullness of the goodness of God.

DIFFERENT TYPES OF PRAYER

There are so many different types of prayer and so many different ways to pray. I grew up believing that if I was going to pray, I had to use words. I have discovered that is only one form of prayer. There are many other forms of prayer. Often when I am in prayer, I do not use words at all. And sometimes when I am in that place, the Lord brings me into different types of prayer or intercessory experiences where the way that I pray begins to change. I do not go seeking these experiences out, but sometimes when I am in that place, they come upon me. Some of those different types of prayer include travail, brooding, ecstasies, and types of contemplative prayer.

TRAVAIL

One type of prayer is travail. Travail is a type of prayer where a person "labors" in prayer. A great example of travail is what Jesus did in the Garden of Gethsemane. In Luke 22:44 it says, *"Being in agony, He prayed more earnestly. Then his sweat became like great drops of blood falling down to the ground."* Travail is an intense feeling of giving birth to something. During travail, your prayers are deep cries and groans that come from your inner man. There are times when all that you can do is act out in a physical way what is happening in the spirit realm. These physical acts become prophetic. They become the very thing that will cause a release to come in what you are praying for.

It may be easier to describe what travail is with an example. One evening at church, Bill and I both noticed one of the young ladies who was having a difficult time. At the time, she was in close relationship with someone who had been diagnosed with cancer. The young lady came over to us and began to cry and shake. I knew immediately that she was moving into travail. I knew it was not something that she had picked because it is not in her personality at all. I explained to her what was happening and told her that she was in travail. I prayed with her through the entire process and let her travail through the rest of the worship service. I sat with her as deep groans came up out of her. After a little while, I knew that she needed to be released from the travail, and I told her to release the prayer burden that she was experiencing back to God. As soon as she released the burden back to God, you could see the release come over her. The young lady asked me if she could use one of the flags and go up on the platform. This was so out of character for her that I knew it was God. She went up on stage and used the flag as worship. When she did this, I felt like there was a release for her and that this was something she needed to do—something in the physical realm as the fruit of what had just happened in the spiritual realm. She did not carry that travail or the heaviness anymore; she had released it and given it to God.

Let me give you another example of travail. James Goll, an itinerant minister, was visiting our church years ago for a conference. During the conference, James came up to me and called me a weeping intercessor. At that point in my life, it was like refreshing water to my spirit to hear those words. He was right when he called it out to me. I felt like that was all I was doing, just crying in travail all of the time. I was asking God, "Why am I doing all this crying?" Many of us feel God in different ways. And sometimes we show physical manifestations

> *Feeling His love for this world is a very intense feeling and will undo you every time.*

of those feelings. When I feel God, I usually cry. It could have been because I was feeling His joy and I was crying tears of joy, or sometimes I was feeling His strong presence and His desire or His love for the world. Feeling His love for this world is a very intense feeling and will undo you every time. His love is vast and great and those words don't come close to describing His love for us.

Sometimes, when a person is in travail, it can almost appear as if she is in the process of childbirth. I remember a lot of people were falling into travailing prayer during the late '90s when there was so much change that was taking place in the spiritual atmosphere of the Church. I could feel it all. It was amazing to feel and see what God was doing. It was a pushing in the spiritual realm. At the church, we were having prayer meetings during the week. There were meetings that were filled with travail and great celebration. People in the church could feel what was happening. I don't know if we understood all that was happening, but we knew that God was doing something really big. There were physical prophetic acts of labor at times in these meetings. It looked as though they were birthing the things of the Lord in their prayers. Some people would have what we affectionately called "the crunches." In one of our services I remember there were several of us women who began to double over with labor type symptoms. It looked like we were having contractions.

During that season, we spent hours laughing and crying together. Little did we know what God would be establishing in the years to come. We felt it but didn't have complete definition for it.

Travail is a deep calling in your spirit. Everything in you is exploding with groanings that words can't express. It shakes your very core. Psalm 42:7 says:

Deep calls to deep at the sound of Your waterfalls;
All Your breakers and Your waves have rolled over
me (NASB).

Think about this verse. God's sound, like waterfalls, has called you to the deep place; all of His breakers and waves roll over you. If and when this happens, you become a mess. You become a complete mess for God. It makes you cry out for God all the more. Unfortunately, some people can let themselves stay in that place of travail long after the Lord has called them to it. If they are not careful, they can and will carry the feelings of that realm and turn them into soul feelings, which will only lead to sorrow. I can't tell you how many intercessors have ended up consumed by worldly sorrow. We have to understand that the devil does not play fair. He will take a very anointed time and twist it and turn it, and you will find yourself in a state of depression because you carried sorrow for too long. In short, something birthed by the Spirit can become fleshly if we are not careful.

BROODING

There are times when the Holy Spirit gives us specific things to pray for. And they won't go away. That is brooding, a type of prayer where we "sit on" or "ponder over" an issue that we are praying about.

I thought I would use this prayer tool one day when I had a mother come to me and ask for prayer for her son who was in prison. He needed God. So I shared with her about this brooding of the Holy Spirit. We prayed and asked that the Holy Spirit would come and brood over and around him, to cause life to come to him. A short time after that, she came back to me and told me that her son had given his life to the Lord. I remember thinking, "That was fast." So, I began using that whenever a parent would come and ask for prayer for a child. On one occasion, I had a father come who was so broken over his daughter's choices for her life. She had turned away from God. As we prayed, we released the Holy Spirit to come and brood over her so that she would feel the presence of the Holy Spirit. He came to me the next week with a great report. He had met with her after a week, and they went for a walk. She opened up and told him, "I don't know what you did, Dad, but I have felt God this week. It is like He is right next to me."

When the Holy Spirit "moves" over void, empty things, life can be the only result. When we are in this place of brooding, we stay very focused in our prayers. We are driven by Heaven to see an answer come.

> *The earth was without form, and void; and darkness was on the face of the deep. And the Spirit of God was hovering over the face of the waters* (Genesis 1:2).

When we brood, we bring the issues "under our wings" so to speak and keep them close to our hearts and pray until the birth comes. In his book *Intercessory Prayer*, Dutch Sheets gives a great word study on the word *hovering*.[1] It is a creative word. When the Holy Spirit "hovered" or "moved" or "brooded over," it produced life where there was void, nothingness. The word *hover* is used as a term for when a hen broods over her chicks.

BABY CHICKS

Let me tell you a story to illustrate this brooding prayer. Years ago, when our children were young, we decided that we would raise some chickens. It was so much fun. The kids and I would race to the pen to see how many eggs we could collect. One morning I noticed that one of the hens was sitting on her eggs. So every morning, we would look inside the nest to see the progress. We were so excited and waited anxiously for the new chicks. One very cold morning as I walked into the pen, the mama hen stood up and out from her wings fell two little chicks. She had birthed them, and they were amazing. I think about that picture often when it comes to prayer.

Many times that is what we are doing when we intercede. We are brooding over something, causing life to come. I never saw those eggs while that mama was sitting. They were hidden away. It was a secret place. That hen was protecting those chicks with all of her might. Can you see the joy of anticipation in the brooding process? Yes it's work and it takes endurance, but there is an excitement because you know that the answer is coming. That mama hen just sat and waited. We do the same. We wait and protect, creating the atmosphere that enables the birth to happen. What joy!

Cause and Effect

I had a friend come to me and tell me that she saw that I was praying for three things. The picture she saw was of a hen that was brooding over her eggs. When she told me this, it helped me identify what I was feeling about three different things that I had been praying about. I was producing or creating something in my prayers that was causing life to come, that was causing an answer. It's cause and effect. Cause and effect—the way perspectives, objectives, and/or measures interact in a series of cause-and-effect relationships—demonstrates the impact of achieving an outcome. You are the right person at the right time causing increase as you pray. Many times intercessors feel that they are hovering over an issue that the Father is birthing in them. They can actually feel the life coming as they pray.

Sometimes the Holy Spirit will have us "brood over" a topic that we are praying about. For me, a lot of the things that I find myself "brooding over" are issues of more global concern. When this happens, God will release prayer strategies to me little by little, and I will sit on that thing until I see the answer. And I know when it has been "birthed" because I see the answer come. Sometimes, what I see is a process of answers or a progression of answered prayer. For example, sometimes I will hear about an answer of something that I have been brooding over in a news story or in a casual conversation. I make sure that, when I am brooding over something, I continually look for an answer because I know that God always answers my prayers. I expect it.

BREATH PRAYERS

There are some prayers that seem to come up out of your inner self. I call these breath prayers. They're not long prayers, but they are spirit-breathed. Many times when I soak in God's presence, I will experience this breath. It will start deep inside of me and stir me to where my own breath is taken away. Many times there are no words that come, only breathing Him in and breathing my prayers out.

A THIN PLACE

A thin place is a place where Heaven and earth are close. It is easier to experience the spiritual realm in these places. A lot of times, you can tell when you are in a "thin place" because there are a lot of spiritual or creative people who are gathered there. Examples of this include Sedona, Arizona; Ashland, Oregon; and many parts of Ireland, which is known for its thin places. In contemplative prayer, you discover that the atmosphere around you becomes thin to the point that there is no division between Heaven and earth. A friend and I were walking down a trail one day to visit a water site that we wanted to pray at. We were praying as we walked. Both of us at the same time ran right into a thin place. We both stopped and said, "Wow. Do you feel that?"

We felt like we had just entered into a place where our world and the realm of Heaven collided. We got so drunk in the Spirit from walking into that thin place that we could hardly make it the rest of the way down the trial.

DARK NIGHT OF THE SOUL

There are times in our lives that we go through really hard stuff. We can do one of two things: run away from God or run to Him. I've found that running to Him is the only answer. During this dark night of the soul God allows us to come to a brokenness that brings us to complete surrender. If we turn to Him in surrender and release everything to Him, a peace will come and settle deep in us. It will feel like an oil of healing being poured over and in us. The sweetness of this peace will take away the brokenness.

There are other times that we are in great travail over something. The burden of this can feel so overpowering that we feel as though we could die. These are times that we need to stay very close and continually give Him the burden. We need to turn the dark night of the soul over to Him. The world doesn't need our sadness; they need our joy.

ECSTASIES

An *ecstasy* could be defined as a period of time in prayer when the awareness of the soul is suspended and the only focus that the person has is the incredible presence of the Lord.

Sometimes my only prayer is, "God I want to be one with you." The only desire of my heart is to know Him and be known by Him. When I am in that place, sometimes I find myself slipping into the ecstasies of God. When I slip into the ecstasies of God, I slip into an eternal realm where I become so consumed by the presence of God that it feels like I cease to exist outside of His goodness. In that place, I become completely consumed by

Him. In that place, I become completely known by Him. In that place, I become one with Him.

One mystic who was often swept up into "ecstasies" was St. Teresa of Avila. Author of (among other books and writings) *Interior Castle*, a classic book about union with God and contemplative prayer, Teresa of Avila was a Spanish mystic who lived from 1515-1582. Here is how she described her experience of union with God:

> It pleased our Lord that I should see the following vision a number of times. I saw an angel near me, on the left side, in bodily form. This I am not wont to see, save very rarely.... In this vision it pleased the Lord that I should see it thus. He was not tall, but short, marvelously beautiful, with a face which shone as though he were one of the highest of the angels, who seem to be all of fire: they must be those whom we call Seraphim.... I saw in his hands a long golden spear, and at the point of the iron there seemed to be a little fire. This I thought that he thrust several times into my heart, and that it penetrated to my entrails. When he drew out the spear he seemed to be drawing them with it, leaving me all on fire with a wondrous love for God. The pain was so great that it caused me to utter several moans; and yet so exceeding sweet is this greatest of pains that it is impossible to desire to be rid of it, or for the soul to be content with less than God.[2]

CONTEMPLATIVE PRAYER

Contemplative prayer is an inner prayer, a spirit-to-spirit prayer, a form of meditation, a dwelling on Him. I could also define contemplative prayer as an awareness of God. A lot of the different types of prayer already mentioned in this book are types of contemplative prayer. When I am in a place of contemplative prayer, I would say that I am in a place where I am aware of the presence of God.

I find myself falling into contemplative prayer when I quiet myself before God, and I start by just adoring Him. For me, I simply behold the goodness of God, and I find myself slipping away with Him. I don't get there by stress or striving; it is simply by surrendering to His presence.

> Reading seeks, meditation finds (meaning), prayer demands, contemplation tastes (God).
>
> Reading provides solid food, meditation masticates (chews); prayer achieves a savor; contemplation is the sweetness that refreshes.
>
> Reading is on the surface; meditation gets to the inner substance; prayer demands by desire; contemplation experiences by delight. —Teresa of Avila[3]

Some people, when contemplating God, will take a verse or word pertaining to God, like His greatness, and begin to meditate on it. As they put themselves in this quiet place, they begin to have an awareness of God and His presence indwelling them. This is where words aren't important anymore; it's communication of the Spirit kind. There are many who, from this place, will begin to have heavenly experiences.

MEDITATION

Formal Christian meditation began with the early Christian monastic practice of reading the Bible slowly. Monks would carefully consider the deeper meaning of each verse as they read it. This slow and thoughtful reading of Scripture, and the ensuing pondering of its meaning, was their meditation. This spiritual practice is called "divine reading," or lectio divina.

> Sometimes the monks found themselves sponta-neously praying as a result of their meditation on Scripture, and their prayer would in turn lead on to a simple, loving focus on God. This wordless love for God they called contemplation.
>
> The progression from Bible reading, to meditation, to prayer, to loving regard for God, was first formally described by Guigo II, a Carthusian monk and prior of Grande Chartreuse in the 12th century. Guigo named the four steps of this "ladder" of prayer with the Latin terms lectio, meditatio, oratio, and contemplatio.[4]

All of these people had the same thing in common: a passion and fire within to seek after God. We can't be afraid to enter this realm with God. We can't be afraid that it might be some-thing demonic. For years in the Church, meditation has been misunderstood as something that belongs only to different cults. Listen, many of the things in cults are just perversions of the real. The practice of meditation, in many cults, is the practice of emptying your head of all things. That is what they call medita-tion. As believers, when we meditate on the Lord, we are actu-ally filling our heads with the wonders of God and His greatness.

> *Be angry, and do not sin. Meditate within your heart on your bed, and be still. Selah* (Psalm 4:4).

By now you have figured out that having an intimate rela-tionship with the Three-ness, the Holy Trinity, is vital in an intercessor's life. We must learn to know the Father, the Son, and the Holy Spirit. Being righteous is being in right standing with God, the Trinity. The Bible says that the effective, fervent prayers of a righteous man avails (profits) much (see James 5:16). The Message Bible says it this way: *"The prayer of a person living right with God is something powerful to be reckoned with."* We must have an ongoing relationship with the Trinity and be constant in our pursuit of this heavenly presence. We must experience the Godhead.

LOSE YOURSELF IN HIM

All of the words in this book come down to one thing: time spent with God. There is a place in all of us that cannot be filled with anything but God. It's a deep place for us to dwell with our heavenly Father. In order for us to get to this place, we must quiet ourselves inside and learn to know and feel Him.

Tonight, as you lay your head on your pillow, let all of the stuff from your day just fall off, and begin to think on Him. Meditate in your heart about His goodness. Read a verse or pick a word that describes Him and begin to connect your spirit with His. Take some time and practice being still before Him. Words won't be necessary. One of the proposed meanings of the word *selah* is "to pause and ponder." Ponder the things of God. As you practice this, you will soon be lost and caught up in His presence. You will begin to understand His world.

About Bill and Beni Johnson

Bill and Beni Johnson are the Senior Pastors of Bethel Church. Together they serve a growing number of churches that have partnered for revival. Beni oversees Bethel's intercessors and Prayer House. Her approach to intercession makes supernatural connection with the Lord accessible to all. Bill and Beni have three children and their spouses. They also have eight grandchildren.

ENDNOTES

1. Dutch Sheets, *Intercessory Prayer* (Ventura, CA: Regal Books, 1996), 157.

2. Teresa of Avila, quoted in Allison E. Peers, *Studies of the Spanish Mystics, Vol. 1* (New York: The Macmillan Co., 1927), 197.

3. "Teresa of Avila Lectio," http://www.prayingchurch.org/teresa.html; accessed April 13, 2008.

4. "Christian Meditation," http://en.wikipedia.org/wiki/Christian_meditation; accessed April 13, 2008.

Chapter 4

HEALING AND INTERVENTIONAL ANSWERS

by Elmer L. Towns

WHEN GOD SUPERNATURALLY HEALS

Charles Hughes was an outstanding upperclassman at Liberty University who was called into evangelism. God's power had rested upon him, for he preached in some of the largest churches in America (over 5,000 in attendance) and had great results in souls saved, yet he was still an undergraduate at Liberty University.

Charles was traveling to an evangelistic crusade in Harrisburg, Pennsylvania, in 1978 when the van in which he was riding was hit by an eighteen-wheeler semi and was completely demolished. Charles' head was crushed and to save his life the doctors removed the top of his skull because of intense internal swelling of the brain.

After doing everything possible, the doctors told Jerry Falwell and his father, Dr. Robert Hughes, Dean of Liberty Theological Seminary, that Charles would die. The doctors asked the family if they would sign papers to donate his organs to living recipients. The medical community felt that Charles was as good as dead.

When faced with this emergency, Falwell called a day of fasting and prayer by the entire ministry family of Liberty University and Thomas Road Baptist Church. Some advised Jerry not to do it because Charles was "as good as dead."

But Jerry believed prayer and fasting would save Charles' life. The following night at Thomas Road Baptist Church auditorium Jerry announced, "I am so sure that Charles will be healed, that I am inviting him to be the speaker at Liberty's graduation this year." At that time, graduation was only five months away, and Charles was hanging on to a faint sliver of life.

Sometimes God gives an inner assurance—supernatural faith—that He's about to do something great. This is called *"the prayer of faith that will save the sick"* (James 5:15 PEB). A prayer of faith is being absolutely sure the answer will come before it happens.

> *A prayer of faith is being absolutely sure the answer will come before it happens.*

Five months later, Charles sat on the platform with Jerry Falwell, a huge bandage around his head. The day's greatest miracle was Charles himself, not the results of the message that he was going to bring. Sadly, much of the power that Charles had as a young man was lost. His message was average, but everyone present agreed that the greatest miracle that day was that Charles was alive. The event was electrified. God honored the faith of the entire Thomas Road Baptist Church family and Liberty student body. Today, Charles has gone on to earn his bachelor's, master's, and doctorate degrees.

And what does Charles do today for ministry? He is in charge of the Prayer Room at Liberty University. He doesn't have to say much to encourage students to pray; just his life in the Prayer Room is a testimony to all that "God answers prayers."

LET'S PRAY NOW

When you begin to pray for someone who needs healing, examine whether they are sick because of sin in their life. Notice the promise of healing is attached to the condition of confessing sin and getting forgiveness, *"The prayer of faith shall save the sick...and if he has committed sins he will be forgiven,* [therefore] *confess your trespasses"* (James 5:15-16 PEB). Why does the Bible connect sickness to sin? For two reasons: First, because certain sins cause physical illness. We know that cigarette smoking leads to cancer, and excessive alcohol drinking leads to cirrhosis of the liver, and a sexually filthy lifestyle can lead to AIDS. Therefore, sin can be the direct cause of a person's illness, or it can be an indirect cause through circumstances that bring about illness—sin destroys a person's self-discipline and/or cleanliness, so that a filthy lifestyle introduces germs and infections into the body. Second, their illness is a judgment of God. On another occasion, *"Many are weak and sick among you..."* (1 Cor. 11:30 PEB).

So the sick person must deal with their sins for healing. Notice again the passage says, *"Confess your trespasses one to another...that you may be healed"* (James 5:16 PEB). Sins must be dealt with before God will administer healing.

James introduced the section on praying for sick people by pointing us to the consequences of sin, *"lest you fall into judgment"* (James 5:12 PEB).

The elders of the church must be involved in praying for healing. James tells us, *"...call for the elders..."* (James 5:14 PEB). Why elders and not a traveling evangelist, or some other person?

Because elders have spiritual oversight of the flock of God, and they probably know of any sin or rebellion in the life of the sick person that led to his or her illness. Because elders have the command to *"shepherd the flock"* (1 Peter 5:2 PEB), they must know their flock to exercise "watch-care" over their flock, and pray for those in their flock. Therefore, based on their spiritual relationship to the sick person, they can provide healing for the soul before they provide prayer for the body. Perhaps many who have prayed for healing didn't get it because they left out the ministry of their local church.

When you pray for healing, you are asking God to give the person spiritual and physical life. Remember, the Bible teaches, *"Every good gift and every perfect gift is from above,"* (James 1:17 PEB). Therefore, it is God who gives good health.

> ### Good health comes from God, but it also comes from the body.

Good health comes from God, but it also comes from the body. The body has the ability to heal itself. A doctor, medicine, or any other therapy doesn't really heal the person. The body heals itself. A doctor may prescribe a medicine to eliminate a cause of illness—germs, infections, or other causal factors. Also a doctor may cut away infection in surgery. But in the final analysis, the body heals itself. So when you pray for someone's healing, you're praying for something the body is already trying to do—get well.

When you pray for healing, you should also ask God to reveal any unknown or unseen factors that cause sickness. Maybe a doctor has not made the patient any better. Maybe there's something that causes a person to be sick that hasn't been treated. Your responsibility is to pray for insight to discover what caused the illness.

When I was teaching at Trinity Evangelical Divinity School in the late '60s, I had a colleague who became very sick and the medical community was unable to discover the cause of the illness. But after a day or two in the hospital, he got well and went back to work.

This happened a couple of times, and only when he was hospitalized did he get better.

Then the entire family came down with the same symptoms, they stopped praying for healing, and began asking God to reveal the unseen cause of their physical problems. Shortly thereafter, they discovered that a beautiful set of China cups that had been given to them had not been thoroughly fired in a kiln to seal the ceramic finish. The lead paint melted in the hot tea, and they were unknowingly poisoning themselves. So how did God heal the family? By helping them discover the cause of their sickness.

Pray for God to effectively use the drugs and/or therapy described by the physician. The same with exercise and physical therapy. Pray for the revitalization of the body when therapy is used.

Don't be discouraged if God doesn't answer your prayer for healing. It's not God's will that everyone be healed. Remember, Paul prayed three times for God to take away his *"thorn in the flesh,"* but God didn't answer that request (2 Cor. 12:8 PEB). Also, Paul said he left Trophimus sick in Miletum (2 Tim. 4:20 PEB). Even Jesus didn't heal every sick person He met. He encountered a great multitude at the Pool of Bethesda (see John 5:3 PEB), but He only healed one man who had been lame for 38 years (see John 5:5-9 PEB). On another occasion, Jesus cured all who came to see Him (see Matt. 12:15 PEB), but on another occasion, *"they brought to Him all who were sick"* and *"He healed many who were sick with various diseases"* (Mark 1:32,34 PEB). Did you see that *all* were brought, but He healed only *many*? That suggests Jesus did not heal all.

Finally, the key to healing is not your faith, nor is it the severity of the sick person. Healing power is with God. When you exercise the "prayer of faith," remember it is faith in the source of healing—God—that you must recognize, not faith in your prayer, or even faith in your faith. You must have faith in what God can do.

> *Since God can do all things, God can heal anyone.*

Since God can do all things, God can heal anyone. But since God doesn't do everything that is asked of Him, but He only does His will; then let's pray in the will of God. Let's pray *"not My will, but Yours be done"* (Luke 22:42 PEB).

Praying for $35 Million

In 1998 I was sitting in a planning committee meeting for Billy Graham's training committee called *Amsterdam 2000*. Billy planned to bring together 10,000 evangelists from 235 nations of the earth. While all would be asked to pay their own expenses, most of them could not attend without significant subsidy. The conference would raise funds to help to pay their expenses to Amsterdam, Netherlands, including airfare, food, and accommodations for 10 days.

"I want to train them to do evangelism, just like I do it," Billy said to the 16 of us through John Corts, the Executive Director of the Billy Graham Evangelistic Association. So we were seeking to invite only evangelists who proclaim the good news of Christ, urge a personal response to Christ, and provide nurture to incorporate new believers into local church fellowships.

Billy said, "My greatest legacy is not a school of evangelism with my name on it, but to have 10,000 evangelists doing soul-winning the way I understand evangelism, but doing it in their own native tongue within their cultural expressions of their native home."

Previously, Billy had organized *Amsterdam '83* for 3,000 participants and *Amsterdam '86* for another 6,000 itinerant evangelists. It had cost $35 million. Now, 13 years later we were planning to train 10,000 more evangelists and there had been 13 years of inflation. But after skillful planning and careful budgeting that incorporated what was learned from previous mistakes and experience, the committee felt it could put on *Amsterdam 2000* for the same per person cost of $3,500, or $35 million for 10,000 participants.

> **INTERVENTIONAL ANSWERS:**
> *Interventional answers are when we want God to remove a serious barrier to His work or provide a miraculous supply of resources.*

I choked at the amount because I am not a great man of faith.

I knew how hard it was to raise money—mass mailings, radio appeals, pledge cards, myriad phone calls, visits, and contacts, repeating the story, and asking for contributions. I thought to myself, "It's not easy to raise thirty-five million dollars. I've never seen Jerry Falwell go after that much money."

Then we were told, "Billy said, 'It'll be easy.'" The opposite of what I thought.

"I'll write and ask thirty-five thousand people to give me $1,000 each." He went on to explain, "There are about that many people who have, over the years, each given $1,000 or more to the Billy Graham Evangelistic Association."

Then he added, "It may be as simple as writing a letter to 35,000 people and trusting God to touch their hearts and enable them to support the vision."

Then I impulsively raised my hand, "I'll give the first $1,000."

What was insurmountable to me was a simple faith statement to Billy Graham. He believed God could supply millions of dollars because it included carrying out the call of God upon his life. Billy believed God could provide $35 million because it would lead to winning souls to Christ.

LET'S PRAY NOW

It's all right to ask for big extraordinary things, but make sure the thing for which you ask is God's will. Search your heart to make sure you are not asking for selfish reasons, or for your ease, riches, or glory. You must ask for things that are the will of God.

First, you must have confidence that *your prayers are based on God's will. "This is confidence...that if we ask according to His will He hears us, and we know when He hears us, we have the answers we seek of Him"* (1 John 5:14-15 ELT). You find God's will in God's Word. Sometimes it is God's will that a person dies just as it may be God's will for you to fail so He can lead you in another direction. Paul prayed three times for healing but didn't get it (see 2 Cor. 12:8-9 PEB).

Second, you must *be careful not to ask something that God has not promised in His Word.* Jesus tells us, *"If you abide in Me, and My words abide in you, you will ask what you desire, and it shall be done for you"* (John 15:7 PEB).

According to this verse, there are three things that get your prayers answered: 1) you must be abiding in Jesus, which means you have yielded yourself to Him, 2) God's Word must control your thinking and asking, and 3) you must ask to receive. Therefore, your prayers will be answered when you ask for things promised by the Bible.

Third, you must *tie your request to fasting and continual prayer.* Jesus said, *"...if you have faith...you will say to this mountain...*

move...and it will move.... However, this kind does not go out except by prayer and fasting" (Matt. 17:20-21 PEB).

Can we really expect God to respond if we don't invest an enormous amount of time and agony in prayer? Just making a bold request doesn't move mountains.

So what must we do? We must make bold *faith requests* from the very depths of our beings. We must pray with all our hearts, giving up sleep for an all-night prayer meeting. We must fast and pray for a day, or for a week, or for 40 days. We must sacrifice because we know God *can* answer and we must keep praying until God *does* answer.

> *We must sacrifice because we know God can answer and we must keep praying until God does answer.*

A casual request rolling off our tongues doesn't move God; but God responds when we pray so diligently that we cry and weep. So let me ask, when's the last time you begged God for something?

Fourth, because *we know God can answer, we never quit*. We keep praying even when everything seems black. A strong, bold *faith request* is not something we pray once and then forget. No! When our faith tells us that the answer will come, we can't quit. We ask for it when we get up in the morning and when we pray at a meal. We ask for it while driving around our city, and we ask for it right before we go to sleep. We keep praying, because we believe in a personal God who is guiding us to make extraordinary requests.

The fifth principle is *not doubting in the dark what God has shown us in the light*. The condition for answers is to *"not doubt in his heart...he will have whatever he says"* (Mark 11:23 PEB). We can't work up confidence in the flesh. Neither does it come from circumstances. Confidence comes from God who has the ability to answer.

About Dr. Elmer Towns

Dr. Elmer Towns, vice president of Liberty University, college and seminary professor, dean of the School of Religion, is also the author of numerous popular and scholarly works. He is the recipient of the coveted Gold Medallion Award awarded by the Evangelical Christian Publishers Association for the Book of the Year, *The Names of the Holy Spirit*. He and Ruth, his wife of 56 years, have three children and ten grandchildren.

Chapter 5

PRAYER THAT TAKES HOLD OF THE IMPOSSIBLE!

by Morris Cerullo

...If ye have faith as a grain of mustard seed; ye shall say unto this mountain, Remove hence to yonder place; and it shall remove; and nothing shall be impossible to you (Matthew 17:20 KJV).

Prayer is, without a doubt, the most powerful force on earth. It is unlimited and unsurpassed in its scope and power.

Prayer knows no boundaries and is not limited by time or space.

R.A. Torrey very eloquently and powerfully said concerning the power of prayer:

Prayer can do anything God can do. All that God is and all that God has is at the disposal of prayer.

Through prayer we are transported into the heavenlies where we stand before Almighty God in His glorious majesty, seated upon His Throne. We are able, through prayer, to tap into the unlimited power of God and take hold of the impossible. The vast, unsearchable resources of Heaven are at our disposal through prayer!

God has given us *"...exceeding great and precious promises; that by these ye might be partakers of the divine nature..."* (2 Pet. 1:4 KJV). There are approximately 37,000 promises in God's Word! From Genesis to Revelation, God has given us His promises, which make provision for every need in every area of our lives to be met.

> **By His promises, God puts all things He possesses into our hands. Prayer and faith put us in possession of this boundless inheritance.**
>
> **—E.M BOUNDS**

By His promises, He has placed all things He possesses in our hands. Prayer and faith enable us to take possession of those promises and appropriate them in our lives. We can have all that God has!

Prayer can transcend the laws of nature, invade the realm of the dead, and restore life. Prayer can give instant access to anywhere: into any home, hospital, office, courtroom, prison cell, or any other location desired.

I will never forget when my darling wife, Theresa, was at the point of death. She had been at death's door several times but God healed her. One day in a Partners' Conference a man came up to us and said, "Theresa, honey, is everything all right?" Theresa answered, "Yes, it is now." He said, "Well, on such and such a day God woke me up and for three days I prayed and interceded for you." Those were the three days Theresa had hovered between life and death.

Through prayer, entrance can be gained into nations of the world considered "closed" to the Gospel. Nothing can stop or hinder entrance into communist-controlled areas such as North Korea, Vietnam, or remote villages hidden away in the jungles of Africa or South America. God has given us a secret weapon called prayer that gives us access to anywhere in the world!

Your prayers can be used by God to impact cities and nations, bring salvation, healing, and deliverance to people in India, Africa, China, Indonesia, Saudi Arabia, or any other country.

Through prayer, angels can be brought down to protect you and your family.

Your prayers can go into a hospital operating room and help guide the surgeon's hands and release a flow of God's healing power into a loved one.

The following is a true story about a minister who was in critical condition in a San Francisco hospital. For several days he hung between life and death, experiencing excruciating pain in his leg. The ministers of his denomination were in a conference and were called to pray for him. In the middle of their session, they knelt as a group and began to pray earnestly for him. At that exact moment, the pain left his body.

A day or two later he lost consciousness and had a vision of Heaven. As he talked with Jesus in this vision, he saw two ministers, one standing on each side of him. They were two of his best friends who were in Los Angeles interceding for him at that very moment. Although they were in Los Angeles, physically separated by many miles, through prayer they were at his side.

ABSOLUTELY NOTHING IS IMPOSSIBLE THROUGH PRAYER!

You can live in a dimension of powerful, penetrating prayer where nothing is impossible to you. It may be difficult to understand, but it is true. This is not just an empty statement or spiritual jargon to make one feel good. It is God's promise based upon His Word.

Jesus said:

> ...*If ye have faith as a grain of mustard seed; ye shall say unto this mountain, Remove hence to yonder place; and it shall remove; and nothing shall be impossible to you* (Matthew 17:20 KJV).

Jesus later emphasized this power of doing the impossible when He cursed the fig tree and it dried up according to His Word.

> ...*If you have faith, and do not doubt, you shall not only do what was done to the fig tree, but even if you say to this mountain, "Be taken up and cast into the sea," it shall happen. And all things you ask in prayer, believing, you shall receive* (Matthew 21:21-22 NASB).

Jesus said that if you have faith and do not doubt, "all things you ask in prayer, believing, you shall receive." When He said "all," He didn't mean one or two things. He didn't mean 50 percent of the things we ask for. He meant what He said. All means 100 percent!

Six times in His final hours with His disciples, Christ emphasized the unlimited extent of prayer using the all-inclusive words: "all things," "anything," "whatsoever," "all things whatsoever."

These promises are great and the possibilities of prayer are vast, yet the majority of Christians today have not been able to take hold of them and are living far below what God has provided for them. The Church, as a whole, seems almost unaware of the power that God has placed into its hands.

The unlimited possibilities of prayer are linked to the infinite and omnipotent power of God. There is nothing too hard for Him. He has said; *"Behold, I am the Lord, the God of all flesh: is there any thing too hard for Me?"* (Jer. 32:27 KJV).

Christ has promised, *"For everyone that asketh receiveth; and he that seeketh findeth; and to him that knocketh it shall it be opened"* (Matt. 7:8 KJV). God has bound Himself to us with His Word and He will not withhold anything from faith and prayer. As our Father, He finds the greatest pleasure in answering and meeting our needs. Jesus said, *"...How much more shall your Father which is in heaven give good things to them that ask Him?"* (Matt. 7:11 KJV).

God has chosen to place Himself and all He has at our disposal and directs us to ask. He has said, *"...Ask Me of things to come concerning My sons, and concerning the work of My hands command ye Me"* (Isa. 45:11 KJV).

> ***Do not bring before God small petitions and narrow desires and say, "Lord, do according to these." Ask for great things, for you are before a great throne.***
>
> **—CHARLES SPURGEON**

God is sovereign, unlimited, and all-powerful! He has a master plan and is working upon earth to fulfill that plan. He is in control. He is not sitting in the heavens with His hands folded. He is sovereignly working in the lives of men and nations, and He has ordained prayer as a means whereby He will work though His people to accomplish His will on earth. Prayer is the major force through which He works on earth. Our lack of prayer causes us to forfeit His blessings, divine intervention, and provision He would have given had we prayed.

His divine intervention in the circumstances of our lives in meeting the desperate needs in our cities and nations, He has made dependent upon our prayers.

In essence, God is saying to His people: "I have called and ordained you to carry out My work on earth. I have made full provision for all that you need and desire. I am the Creator, the High and Holy One, the great I AM. Whatever you need to fulfill My plan and purposes, ask Me and I will do it. All that you need accomplished, all the provision you need, command Me. I am the Creator of Heaven and earth and everything in it; ask largely. Do not be slack, negligent, or limited in your asking, and I will not be slack or limited in My giving."

THE MASTER KEY TO PRAYER

The master key to prayer is developing a strong relationship with Christ through prayer. To have power with God through prayer, you must live in unbroken fellowship with God. Power in prayer is not a result of man's endeavors, but of the Spirit of the living God! It doesn't matter how loud or how long you pray. It doesn't matter whether you are kneeling, standing, sitting, or lying prostrate on your face before God. It doesn't even really matter concerning the words or terminology you use when you pray.

Just the smallest whisper of a prayer spoken in faith will move God on your behalf.

There are many Christians who believe they must go through some type of "spiritual gyrations" of a set formula of prayer in order for God to release His power in answer to their prayers.

As I have stated many times before, "Power does not travel through words; it travels through relationships!"

The power and effectiveness of your prayers are dependent upon a personal intimate relationship with God. Without a strong relationship that has been built through communion with Him, your prayers are nothing more than mere words. Jesus said, *"If ye abide in Me, and My words abide in you, ye shall ask what ye will, and it shall be done unto you"* (John 15:7 KJV).

> *The great people of earth are the people who pray. I do not mean those who talk about prayer; nor those who say they believe in prayer; nor yet those who can explain about prayer; but I mean those people who take time to pray.*
> —S.D. GORDON

When you have developed a strong relationship with God, where you are living in unbroken fellowship and communion with Him, your prayers become mighty through God to the "pulling down of strongholds."

The apostle Paul told the Corinthians:

> *For though we live in a world, we do not wage war as the world does. The weapons we fight with are not the weapons of the world. On the contrary, they have divine power to demolish strongholds* (2 Corinthians 10:3-4 NIV).

Prayer is a mighty spiritual weapon that God has given you to demolish satan's strongholds. But how is it activated?

Elijah was a mighty man of prayer. He prayed and fire came from God out of Heaven!

He prayed and the dead were raised!

He prayed and the heavens were shut for three and a half years!

He prayed again and the heavens were opened!

For a moment let us look at the prayers Elijah prayed that resulted in a demonstration of the supernatural power of God.

When the son of the widow woman of Zarapheth died, she brought him to Elijah. This woman had seen the miracle power of God released. The cruse of oil and barrel of meal were supernaturally multiplied to meet her need. But when her son died she was overcome with grief and brought him to Elijah.

Imagine that traumatic scene! No doubt the woman was totally distraught, overcome with emotion, weeping and wailing.

Elijah took the boy in his arms and carried him to the room in the widow's house where he was staying. He laid the boy on his bed. Then he began to cry out to God. *"...O Lord my God, hast Thou also brought evil upon the widow with whom I sojourn, by slaying her son?"* (1 Kings 17:20 KJV).

At first, Elijah did not understand why God had allowed the boy to die. This prayer wasn't an expression of Elijah's doubt. It was simply his honest, heartfelt cry.

Elijah knew God intimately. He knew God's unlimited power. As an act of faith, Elijah stretched himself upon the child three times and cried, *"...O Lord my God, I pray Thee, let this child's soul come into him again"* (1 Kings 17:21 KJV).

Elijah did not pray a long, drawn-out prayer. His prayer was simple and direct. It was a prayer of faith based upon his personal knowledge of Almighty God.

God responded to Elijah's heartfelt cry and restored the child's life. *"And the Lord heard the voice of Elijah; and the soul of the child came into him again, and he revived"* (1 Kings 17:22 KJV).

Look at the prayer Elijah prayed when God sent fire from Heaven to consume the sacrifice on the altar. His prayer wasn't to draw attention to himself or to somehow prove he was a man of power. He challenged the prophets of Baal and the children of Israel who had fallen into idolatry and were worshiping Baal. The prophets of Baal and all the people agreed together with him that the God who answered by fire was the one, true, living God.

The power released through Elijah's prayer was the result of his relationship with God. He knew God's power. He knew that God had anointed him as His prophet, and he knew God would answer.

When the time came to offer the evening sacrifice, Elijah stood before the altar and began to pray:

> *...Lord God of Abraham, Isaac, and of Israel, let it be known this day that Thou art God in Israel, and that I am Thy servant, and that I have done all these things at Thy word. Hear me, O Lord, hear me, that this people may know that Thou art the Lord God, and that Thou hast turned their heart back again* (1 Kings 18:36-37 KJV).

God heard Elijah's prayer and answered by sending fire from Heaven. His prayers broke through all natural limitations!

> *Then the fire of the Lord fell, and consumed the burnt sacrifice, and the wood, and the stones, and the dust, and licked up the water that was in the trench* (1 Kings 18:38 KJV).

When God directed Elijah to declare a three and a half year famine, Elijah simply declared,

> *...As the Lord God of Israel liveth, before whom I stand, there shall not be dew nor rain these years, but according to my word* (1 Kings 17:1 KJV).

According to the word Elijah spoke at God's direction, the heavens were shut up. Elijah's prayer transcended the laws of nature! There was no rain or dew and the famine lasted three and a half years. Later, when he prayed for the heavens to be opened, he again prayed according to what God had directed him to do.

> *...The word of the Lord came to Elijah in the third year, saying, Go, shew thyself unto Ahab; and I will send rain upon the earth* (1 Kings 18:1 KJV).

Elijah acted in faith upon the word the Lord spoke to him and went to Ahab. He told Ahab, *"...Get thee up, eat and drink, for there is a sound of abundance of rain"* (1 Kings 18:41 KJV). Elijah wasn't fearful to approach Ahab. He knew the word the Lord had spoken to him would come to pass.

Then Elijah went up to Mount Carmel where he prayed, *"...And he cast himself down upon the earth, and put his face between his knees"* (1 Kings 18:42 KJV).

He told his servant to go and look toward the sea to see if there was any sign of rain. The servant went and looked, but there was no sign of rain. He returned and told Elijah, "There is nothing." Elijah sent his servant a second time. Again, he returned with the same report, "There is nothing."

Elijah did not stop; he persevered in prayer. He sent his servant again and again, a third, fourth, fifth, sixth, and seventh time. On the seventh time the servant returned to Elijah and said, *"...Behold, there ariseth a little cloud out of the sea, like a man's hand"* (1 Kings 18:44 KJV).

The heavens were opened after a three and a half year famine, and there was a great rain in answer to Elijah's prayer.

ELIJAH DID NOT FOLLOW A FORMULA FOR PRAYER

The key to the release of God's power through Elijah's prayer was not because of a "formula" that Elijah followed. It was not because of the words he spoke. It was because of Elijah's relationship with God.

Elijah was not superhuman. He was a man with a nature that was subject to the same feelings, passions, and desires that you and I have. Following his great victory over the prophets of Baal, when God sent fire from Heaven in answer to his prayer, Elijah was fearful and discouraged, and he even asked God to let him die.

> *Elijah was a human being with a nature such as we have [with feelings, affections and a constitution like ourselves] and he prayed earnestly for it not to rain, and no rain fell on the earth for three years and six months. And [then] he prayed again and the heavens supplied rain and the land produced its crops [as usual]* (James 5:17-18 AMP).

Elijah prayed, in faith, according to what God directed him to do. He knew God would do exactly what he said. There was no doubt or wavering.

God has planned for you to have this same power through prayer! James said, *"The prayer of faith shall save the sick..."* (James 5:15 KJV). He said, *"The earnest, (heart-felt, continued) prayer of a righteous man makes tremendous power available [dynamic in its working]"* (James 5:16 AMP).

> *Only divine praying can operate divine promises or carry out divine purposes.*
> —E.M. BOUNDS

93

There are many Christians who pray but are only speaking empty words. They have not developed an intimate relationship with God where they truly know Him and know that He will hear and do all He has promised in His Word. Without this intimate relationship there can be no real power.

YOUR RELATIONSHIP WITH CHRIST IS THE FOUNDATION FOR YOUR POWER IN PRAYER

To become a powerful end-time spiritual warrior, you must also come into a position where you know Christ, where you are one with Him, where you are able to "see" and "hear" in the Spirit what He wants you to do and to say.

One of God's purposes for your life is for you to grow and develop until you come into the *"[full and accurate knowledge] of the Son of God..."* (Eph. 4:13 AMP).

There is only one way that you will be able to do this and that is through prayer!

The only way you will be able to really know Christ in all His fullness is by spending time alone with Him in prayer.

The only way you will be able to know His will for your life is through prayer.

The only way you will be able to penetrate into the realm of the Spirit, where you are able to "see" and "hear" what He wants you to do and to say, is through prayer.

Just as it was necessary for Jesus, in the form of human flesh, to use prayer as a means of communicating with God and knowing His will, it is necessary for you to use prayer as a means of coming into the "full and accurate knowledge" of Jesus.

There is a decision and commitment you must make. Your knowledge of Christ, your relationship, and your union with Him through prayer is the source (the foundation) of your strength. Unless you are willing to discipline your life, as Jesus did, to include consistent times of prayer alone with Him where you are allowing Him to reveal Himself and His will to you, you will not be able to survive.

If you are not willing to make this commitment, if you are not willing to discipline your life, you may as well give up. You are already defeated even before you begin! Unless you have this strong foundation of knowing Christ through prayer, you will not be able to use the other spiritual weapons God has given you.

Take a moment right now to think about the time you are spending each day in prayer. Time when you are getting to know Christ more fully and allowing Him to reveal His will to you. I'm not speaking about the type of prayer where you spend five or ten minutes petitioning God for something or for your loved ones. I am speaking about the type of prayer where you are waiting before Him in His Presence and seeking earnestly to know Him, hungering for Him to reveal Himself to you.

Ask yourself, "How much time am I spending in prayer coming into a full and accurate knowledge of Jesus?"

Are you spending 1 hour...30 minutes...15, 10, or even 5 minutes a day?

Whatever your commitment is right now, increase it. I realize that the demands on your time are great. You may have a family to care for, a job, commitments that fill almost every waking hour. But you must not allow any of these things to crowd out your time alone with Christ.

Regardless of how much time you think you have, increase the amount of time you are now spending in prayer building your relationship with Christ.

As you do this, you will be strengthened. You will be prepared to face every attack of the enemy as Jesus did. As Christ begins to reveal Himself and His will to you during these times of prayer, you will come into a greater knowledge of who He is and who you are as a child of the living God. Jesus said, *"...Whatever the Father does the Son also does"* (John 5:19 NIV). As Christ manifests Himself to you and reveals to you all that He is and does through prayer, you will be able to do the same works!

GOD WILL USE YOU TO SHAPE THE FUTURE THROUGH YOUR PRAYERS

God has established a universal principle concerning His actions being dependent upon our prayers. He has bound Himself to act in response to our prayers. We see this illustrated at the dedication of the Temple. After Solomon prayed, God appeared to him and said:

> *I have heard thy prayer, and have chosen this place to Myself for an house of sacrifice. If I shut up heaven that there be no rain, or if I command the locusts to devour the land, or if I send pestilence among My people; if My people, which are called by My name, shall humble themselves, and pray, and seek My face, and turn from their wicked ways; then will I hear from heaven, and will forgive their sin, and will heal their land. Now Mine eyes shall be open, and Mine ears attent unto the prayer that is made in this place* (2 Chronicles 7:12-15 KJV).

We often quote verse 14 above in relation to prayer and believing God for revival and an outpouring of His Spirit upon our cities and nations. But there is another powerful principle that God wants us to understand.

God told Solomon that whenever he saw the land plagued by drought, locusts, or other pestilences among the people, that through the prayers and repentance of His people, He would heal the land. He would open the heavens and pour out refreshing rain once again. He would drive out the locusts plaguing their crops, and their crops would once again flourish. He would drive out all pestilence from among the people, and they would walk in the fullness of His blessings.

God said their prayers would arise to His Throne and He would hear their cries and would answer. Their prayers would bring His divine intervention upon earth into their circumstances.

God is raising up a people today who understand this powerful universal principle that He has set in motion, making prayer the most powerful force on earth. He has placed everything at our disposal. Every conceivable blessing for our personal lives, families, cities, and nations He has made available and is waiting to release.

> *The power of the Church to truly bless rests on intercession; asking and receiving heavenly gifts to carry to man.*
> —ANDREW MURRAY

He stands ready to intervene in the crises plaguing our world. He longs to reverse the curse of famine, pestilence, sickness, and disease that has come upon the earth through man's sin and disobedience. But He is waiting on the prayers of His people to act.

He is looking for a generation of men and women—intercessors—who will intercede, weep, groan, and travail; who through their prayers will move His hand to intervene upon earth and release His full provision.

God intends you to shape the future through your prayers! The destiny of people and nations are in the hands of His intercessors. God has said, *"And I sought for a man among them, that should make up the hedge, and stand in the gap before Me for the land, that I should not destroy it..."* (Ezek. 22:30 KJV).

God is more than ready to pour out the fullness of His power and blessing. He is speaking to us today, *"Ask Me of things to come concerning My sons, and concerning the work of My hands command ye Me!"* (Isa. 45:11 KJV).

The following is a true story of a woman who believed God and took hold of the impossible. Her husband was in a hospital in Philadelphia in very critical condition. He weighed less than 100 pounds.

His doctor told the wife he was dead. But she said, "No, he is not dead. He cannot be dead. I have prayed for him for twenty-seven years, and God has promised me that he would be saved. Do you think God would let him die now after I have prayed twenty-seven years and God has promised, and he is not saved?"

"Well," the doctor replied, "I don't know anything about that, but I know that he is dead." With that they drew a screen around the bed that, in the hospital separates between the living and the dead.

Seven other physicians were brought in to examine her husband, and all confirmed that he was dead. The woman continued to kneel at the side of her husband's bed insisting that he was not dead—that if he were dead God would bring him back for He had promised her that he would be saved.

The woman asked the nurse for a pillow for her to place under her knees while kneeling at her husband's bedside.

One hour, two hours, three hours passed as she knelt beside the lifeless body of her husband. Four, five, six, thirteen hours passed as she continued kneeling at his side. When they tried to get her to leave, she refused, insisting that God would bring him back from the dead.

At the end of 13 hours her husband opened his eyes and told his wife he wanted to go home. Through prayer she saw her husband raised from the dead and saved by the power of God!

GOD HAS LINKED OUR PRAYERS WITH THE FULFILLMENT OF HIS END-TIME PLAN

Another illustration of the awesome power God has placed in the hands of His people through prayer is found in the Book of Revelation. John was given a glimpse of God seated upon His Throne. Around the throne were 24 elders and four angelic beings, all worshiping God. The Lion of the Tribe of Judah, who appeared as the Lamb of God who had been slain, came forward and took the scroll from the right hand of God.

> *And when he had taken the book, the four living creatures and the twenty-four elders fell down before the Lamb, having each one a harp and golden bowls full of incense, which are the prayers of the saints* (Revelation 5:8 NASB).

Here we see that before the seals and the awesome judgments of God begin, the prayers of God's people are offered up with incense. Our prayers here on earth on behalf of the lost, our cries to Him regarding the wickedness and immorality surrounding us and for God's will and purposes to be fulfilled do not disappear into thin air. They are not forgotten. They ascend before God and are as sweet-smelling incense in His nostrils.

After the last seal is opened, before the judgments of God are poured out upon the earth, there is total silence in Heaven for one-half hour. All of Heaven waits in hushed silence for what will soon be revealed.

Standing before God's Throne is a strong angel holding in his hand a golden censer. The angel is given incense, which he mixes with the prayers of all saints throughout the ages and offers it as an offering to God on the golden altar before the Throne.

The air is permeated with the beautiful fragrance of the prayers, and the cloud of incense surrounds the Throne. *"And the smoke of the incense, which came with the prayers of the saints, ascended up before God out of the angel's hand"* (Rev. 8:4 KJV).

In the same way that Aaron, on the Day of Atonement, took the censer full of burning coals off the altar and went into the Holy of Holies and offered incense before the Mercy Seat, the angel takes the censer with the incense and prayers, and impregnates the air with this holy offering.

The worship in the Tabernacle was to be a type of the heavenly worship. The Mercy Seat was where God appeared in a glory cloud. God directed that Aaron, the High Priest, cover the Mercy Seat with a cloud of incense.

> *And he shall put the incense upon the fire before the Lord, that the cloud of the incense may cover the mercy seat that is upon the testimony, that he die not* (Leviticus 16:13 KJV).

The cloud of incense covering the Mercy Seat in the Tabernacle was symbolic of the cloud of incense mixed with the prayers of God's people that will be offered to God upon His Throne before His judgments are poured out upon the earth.

This heavenly scene reveals the tremendous significance and value that God places upon our prayers.

But, there is more.

In John's vision, after covering the Throne of God with the cloud of incense and prayers, the angel takes the censer, mixes it with fire from off the altar, and casts it down to the earth.

Now, notice the results:

> *...There were voices, and thunderings, and lightnings, and an earthquake* (Revelation 8:5 KJV).

What tremendous force is this that has brought God's power down to earth?

The prayers of God's people!

God has given us this glimpse of how prayer is vitally linked with the fulfillment of His end-time plan. It isn't until the prayers of God's people are offered to Him that the angels are released to sound the trumpets. Then God's judgments come upon the wicked. The angels are God's means of administering the victory, but it will be the saints and their prayers that will win the final victory.

INCENSE...THUNDER...LIGHTNING!

I believe this glorious scene also reveals Heaven's perspective of prayer and what our prayers look like in Heaven. Our prayers today are like incense rising up before God on His Throne. They are mixed with fire from His altar and flung back to earth—as spiritual thunder, lightning, and earthquakes! Our prayers result in God's divine intervention and will being done upon the earth.

David gives us a glimpse of what he saw in the Spirit when he prayed for deliverance in his time of trouble. *"In my distress I called to the Lord; I cried to my God for help. From His temple He heard my voice; my cry came before Him, into His ears"* (Ps. 18:6 NIV).

Now notice what happened as a result of his prayers:

> *The earth trembled and quaked, and the foundations of the mountains shook; they trembled because He was angry. He parted the heavens and came down, dark clouds were under His feet. Out of the brightness of His presence clouds advanced, with hailstones, and bolts of lightning. The Lord thundered from heaven; the voice of the Most High resounded* (Psalm 18:7,9,12-13 NIV).

Earthquake! Lightning! Thunder! This is what David saw in the spirit realm as to how God answered his prayer. He gives us another glimpse into the heavenly realm concerning the awesome power God released in answer to prayer.

In response to David's prayer God began to act. The result was that God delivered him out of the snare of his enemies. David testified of God's answer to his prayer:

> *He rescued me from my powerful enemy, from my foes who were too strong for me. They confronted me in the day of my disaster, but the Lord was my support. He brought me out into a spacious place; He rescued me because He delighted in me* (Psalm 18:17-19 NIV).

A spiritual earthquake, fire, and a mighty wind was released as the incense of the prayers of 120 men and women ascended before God upon His Throne. *"These all continued with one accord in prayer and supplication, with the women, and Mary the mother of Jesus, and with His brethren"* (Acts 1:14 KJV).

In response to their prayers, the Father sent the Holy Spirit in a demonstration of power.

> *And suddenly there came a sound from heaven as of a rushing mighty wind, and it filled all the house where they were sitting. And there appeared unto them cloven tongues like as of fire, and it sat upon each of them. And they were all filled with the Holy Ghost, and began to speak with other tongues, as the Spirit gave them utterance* (Acts 2:2-4 KJV).

Throughout the history of the early Church we see that whenever the Church prayed, incense went up before the Father—spiritual earthquakes, lightning, thunder—God's power was released, resulting in His will being accomplished on earth.

> *And they continued steadfastly in the apostles' doctrine and fellowship, and of breaking of bread,*

and in prayers. And fear came upon every soul: and many wonders and signs were done by the apostles (Acts 2:42-43 KJV).

Are you beginning to see the awesome power and privilege God has given you to partner with Him to bring His power, glory, and will down to earth?

PRAYER THAT BREAKS THROUGH ALL NATURAL LIMITATIONS

Throughout the Word we have an indisputable record of the awesome, unlimited power of prayer. We are surrounded by an innumerable host of witnesses! Let us consider the following who have left a living memorial to God through their answered prayers.

Moses and the children of Israel stood on the banks of the Red Sea. Pharaoh and his great army with their chariots were behind them in hot pursuit. They cried out to God, and He rolled back the Red Sea.

> *To Moses it was given by intercession to place his hand upon God's throne. To you, by grace, it is given to sit with Christ on His throne and there to intercede and prevail for His kingdom.*
> —WESLEY L. DUEWEL

And Moses stretched out his hand over the sea; and the Lord caused the sea to go back by a strong east wind all that night, and made the sea dry land, and the waters were divided. And the children of Israel went into the midst of the sea upon dry ground: and the waters were a wall unto them on their right hand, and on their left (Exodus 14:21-22 KJV).

PRAYER THAT BREAKS THE CHAINS OF DEATH

Prayer knows no boundaries because God is unlimited in power! Prayer can reach into the realm of the dead and break the chains of death!

Elisha's prayers invaded the realm of the dead and raised the Shunammite's son from his deathbed.

> *When Elisha reached the house, there was the boy lying dead on his couch. He went in, shut the door on the two of them and prayed to the Lord. Then he got on the bed and lay upon the boy, mouth to mouth, eyes to eyes, hands to hands. As he stretched himself out upon him, the boy's body grew warm. Elisha turned away and walked back and forth in the room and then got on the bed and stretched out upon him once more. The boy sneezed seven times and opened his eyes* (2 Kings 4:32-35 NIV).

Peter was summoned to Joppa by the disciples to pray for Dorcas who had died. When he arrived at the house, it was filled with mourners. But that did not stop Peter. Peter knew what it was to pray with delegated authority!

> *But Peter put them all forth, and kneeled down, and prayed* (Acts 9:40 KJV).

Notice that after he had prayed, Peter acted in faith. He spoke to Dorcas' dead body!

> *...And turning him to the body said, Tabitha, arise. And she opened her eyes: and when she saw Peter, she sat up. And he gave her his hand, and lifted her up, and when he had called the saints and widows, presented her alive* (Acts 9:40-41 KJV).

Consider Smith Wigglesworth, who ministered from the early 1900s to the 1940s. He was called the "Apostle of Faith" because he believed and preached that God could do the impossible. It is reported that during his ministry 20 people were raised from the dead after he prayed for them.

Smith depended wholly on the Holy Spirit to flow through him. He lived in unbroken communion and fellowship with God and was continuously seeking God's Presence. He said that he never went half an hour without praying. He constantly prayed in tongues.

One day a woman lay at the point of death. She had a tumor, and her body was wracked with pain. An elder from her church, by the name of Mr. Fisher, brought Smith Wigglesworth to pray for her.

Smith told her, "I know you are very weak, but if you wish to be healed and cannot lift your arm, or move it at all, it might be possible that you can raise your finger."

With all the strength she could muster, she focused on raising her finger. Then suddenly, her body went limp and she died.

Mr. Fisher was panic-stricken. "She's dead. She's dead," he cried. He had brought Wigglesworth, hoping that she might be healed, and now she had died.

Wigglesworth pulled back the covers, reached into the bed, and pulled her out. He carried her lifeless body across the room and propped it up against the wall. There was no pulse, no breath. She was dead.

He looked into her face and commanded, "In the name of Jesus, I rebuke this death!" The woman's whole body began to tremble.

"In the name of Jesus, I command you to walk." The woman awoke to find herself walking across her bedroom floor. The pain was gone, and the tumor had disappeared!

Smith Wigglesworth prayed with delegated authority! This is the powerful dimension of prayer that God intends His people to operate in to meet the desperate needs around us today as living proof that He is the one true living God.

PRAYER THAT COMMANDS THE FORCES OF NATURE

Joshua and Isaiah commanded the forces of nature through their prayers!

In the battle against the Amorites for Gibeon, God fought for Israel. He rained hailstones down upon their enemies. Joshua prayed to the Lord and commanded the sun and moon to stand still.

On the day the Lord gave the Amorites over to Israel, Joshua said to the Lord in the presence of Israel:

> *"O sun, stand still over Gibeon, O moon, over the Valley of Aijalon." So the sun stood still, and the moon stopped, till the nation avenged itself on its enemies, as it is written in the Book of Jashar. The sun stopped in the middle of the sky and delayed going down about a full day. There has never been a day like it before or since, a day when the Lord listened to a man. Surely the Lord was fighting for Israel* (Joshua 10:12-14 NIV).

What mighty force commanded the forces of nature and they obeyed?

It was Joshua's prayer.

God heard his prayer and stopped the sun and moon in their courses until Joshua and the children of Israel had avenged themselves on their enemies.

And here's another example: King Hezekiah was at death's door. He cried out to God, and God promised to heal him and add 15 years to his life. Hezekiah requested a sign from Isaiah that he would be healed. The Lord responded:

> *This sign shalt thou have of the Lord, that the Lord will do the thing that He hath spoken: shall the shadow go forward ten degrees, or go back ten degrees? And Hezekiah answered, It is a light thing for the shadow to go down ten degrees: nay, but let the shadow return backward ten degrees* (2 Kings 20:9-10 KJV).

Through his prayer, Isaiah tapped into the unlimited power of God and God turned back time! *"And Isaiah the prophet cried unto the Lord: and he brought the shadow ten degrees backward, by which it had gone down in the dial of Ahaz"* (2 Kings 20:11 KJV).

DARE TO RISE UP AND TAKE HOLD OF THE IMPOSSIBLE THROUGH PRAYER

The power of prayer is unlimited, just as God is unlimited! The major problem in the Church is that we have limited an unlimited God through our lack of knowledge and experience in prayer and through our unbelief.

The record stands true. God has proven Himself faithful to answer the prayers of His people and supernaturally intervene to deliver them out of the hands of their enemies.

When Paul and Silas were beaten and thrown into prison, God heard their prayers. Their prayers and praise arose as incense before the Father, and He responded by sending an earthquake to break their chains and set them free.

> *And at midnight Paul and Silas prayed, and sang praises unto God: and the prisoners heard them. And*

suddenly there was a great earthquake, so that the foundations of the prison were shaken: and imme- diately all the doors were opened, and every one's bands were loosed (Acts 16:25-26 KJV).

What mighty force caused the earth to convulse and the foundations of the prison to shake? The only force on earth pow- erful enough to do this: the prayers of God's servants, Paul and Silas. Their prayers moved the hand of God and brought super- natural deliverance.

The record stands! We read about those mighty warriors of faith:

...who through faith subdued kingdoms, wrought righteousness, obtained promises, stopped the mouths of lions, quenched the violence of fire, escaped the edge of the sword, out of weakness were made strong, waxed valiant in flight, turned to flight the armies of the aliens. Women received their dead raised to life again... (Hebrews 11:33-35 KJV).

What mighty force enabled them to accomplish these great spiritual conquests?

Faith and prayer! Faith and prayer are inseparable. Faith must have a voice to express itself. True prayer is the voice of faith!

From these brief examples, we are able to see the all-encom- passing, unlimited power of prayer and how God has committed Himself into the hands of His people who know Him and have learned how to pray.

LORD, TEACH US TO PRAY!

The unlimited potential of prayer is beyond our natural understanding. But the record remains true. With God all things are possible, and all things are possible to those who know how to prevail with God in prayer.

It is exciting to read about Moses, Elijah, Elisha, Joshua, Peter, and Paul and how God's awesome power was unleashed upon earth through their prayers. God has not changed! He is the same all-powerful, miracle-working God. He doesn't want us to look back. He wants us to remove every limitation we have placed upon Him through our unbelief. He is raising up an end-time army of intercessors today in every nation, who will pray with a powerful, fiery prayer anointing and be used to see cities and nations shaken by His power.

Through their prayers, they will bring God's supernatural power down to earth to meet the desperate needs of the world. They will dare to rise up in faith to take hold of the impossible through prayer.

E.M. Bounds has said concerning the unlimited possibilities of prayer:

> How vast are the possibilities of prayer! How wide its reach! It lays its hand on Almighty God and moves Him to do what He would not do if prayer was not offered. Prayer is a wonderful power placed by Almighty God in the hands of His saints, which may be used to accomplish great purposes and to achieve unusual results. The only limits to prayer are the promises of God and His ability to fulfill those promises.[1]

THE DESTINY OF THE WORLD IS IN THE HANDS OF INTERCESSORS

This is an hour unlike any other. As the Church prepares for the Lord's return, we must by faith begin to tap into the unlimited power of God, through prayer, to see a mighty wave of His power and glory sweep across this world.

Throughout history, every great movement of God's power in revival has come as a result of fervent, prevailing prayer.

During the Great Awakening in the United States in 1857, in one year more than one million people were saved. It began with a man of prayer, Jeremiah Lanphier. He and two other men began to pray for revival. They soon opened a daily noon prayer meeting in the upper room of the Dutch Reformed Church in Manhattan and invited others to join them.

At first only six people showed up. The following week there were 14, and then 23. They started meeting every day and soon filled the Dutch Reformed Church, the Methodist Church, and every public building in downtown New York.

In New York City, 10,000 people a week were saved. The news concerning the prayer meeting spread to outlying cities, and other prayer groups sprang up. After six months, 10,000 businessmen were meeting daily at noon in New York City alone. In eight months, from September until May, 50,000 people in New York City were saved and committed their lives to the Lord.

The move of God spread throughout New England where people would meet to pray three times a day. The revival spread up the Hudson River and down the Mohawk. The fire spread from New York to other cities and then swept over the entire country.

Our whole nation was shaken by the power of God as it had never been shaken before. The revival crossed the Atlantic, broke out in Northern Ireland, Scotland, Wales, England, South Africa, and Southern India.

Four men in Northern Ireland united together and met every Saturday night to pray for revival. They spent the whole night in prayer. God heard their prayers, and the fire of God fell, and revival began to spread across Ireland.

God's power was so strong in some parts of Ireland that courts adjourned because there were no cases to try. Jails were closed because there were no prisoners to incarcerate. Many of the notorious and hardened sinners in the land were converted!

The destiny of cities, nations, people groups, and this world is in the hands of intercessors who will begin to see the unlimited power of prayer. It is in the hands of those who will submit themselves into the hands of God to be used, through their prayers, to bring down His power and a move of His Spirit that will result in a worldwide harvest of souls.

(In Chapter 6 of *How to Pray,* I share God's prophetic purpose for prayer and the position God is calling His intercessors to fill.)

Will you respond to the call of the Spirit?

Will you rise up and take your position in the great army of intercessors that God is mobilizing in this hour to wage war in the heavenlies to bring salvation, healing, and deliverance to a dying world?

LORD, TEACH US TO PRAY!

Dear Father,

Thank You for the awesome power You have made available to us through prayer. Forgive us for limiting You through our unbelief. Open our spiritual eyes to see the unlimited resources You have given us, and how You have chosen to bring Your power and glory down to meet the desperate needs in this world through our prayers. Teach us to pray with new spiritual vision that focuses upon You and Your unlimited power. Break every limitation from our natural minds hindering us from praying prayers that will be used to impact this world and result in a worldwide harvest of souls. We want to build a living memorial to You through answered prayer that will demonstrate to the world that You are the One true living God.

About Dr. Morris Cerullo

Dr. Morris Cerullo has authored more than 160 books. Few ministers have had such an impact on the destiny of the nations of the world. His life has been sacrificially dedicated to training and spiritually equipping pastors, lay people, and evangelists to reach their nations for Christ with a supernatural endowment of God's power.

ENDNOTE

1. E.M. Bounds, *The Classic Collection on Prayer by E.M. Bounds* (Gainsville, FL: Bridge-Logos Publishers, 2002).

Chapter 6

THE
POWER SOURCE

by Suzette T. Caldwell

The grass withers, the flowers fade, but the
Word of our God stands forever (Isaiah 40:8).

My dad came to visit one weekend to see our children play in their basketball and baseball leagues. Instead of Dad having to rent a car, I offered him our family's old Toyota Sequoia. We had purchased a new car, and the Sequoia was just taking up space in the driveway.

A few days before my dad's arrival, my husband decided to fill the tank with gas, take it to the car wash, and get the oil checked. When he turned the ignition the car would not start. He tried it again, but there was no sound. The battery was dead.

After sitting for months, it had lost its charge. Blessedly, a family friend was at the house and she gave the car a jumpstart. In just a few minutes, my husband was on his way.

Like our cars, prayer requires a power source to operate. The power source, or battery, for our prayers is God's Word. Prayer that is loaded with God's Word is charged with life and power. That life and power causes prayer to enter into the supernatural realm, retrieve God's plans for our lives, and bring them back into the natural realm to be manifested as earthly realities.

God's people are required to pray efficacious, powerful prayers. So many Christians have a lackluster, ineffective prayer life because they do not incorporate the Scriptures into their prayers. When you use the Word of God in your prayers, you will experience positive results.

THE AUTHOR OF THE WORD

According to Paul's letter to Timothy, The Word of God was created by God:

> *All Scripture is given by inspiration of God, and is profitable for doctrine, for reproof, for correction, for instruction in righteousness, that the man of God may be complete, thoroughly equipped for every good work* (2 Timothy 3:16-17).

The entire Bible was created by God. There are those people who would like to discredit Scripture by professing it to be full of errors and declaring that it contradicts itself. But the Word of God was never meant to be completely understood by the human mind alone: God gave us the Holy Spirit to help reveal the Bible's meaning and apply it to our lives. It is trustworthy and reliable for us in every area of our lives today (see Ps. 19:7-11).

God is the author of Scripture. The Greek word for "inspira-
tion" found in Second
Timothy 3:16 is *theópneus-*
tos, which means "God-
breathed."[1] Every time God
breathes into or onto something, He infuses it with life.

> *Every time God breathes into or onto something, He infuses it with life.*

Scripture tells us that,
after He created Adam,
God breathed life into his being:

> *And the Lord God formed man of the dust of the*
> *ground, and breathed into his nostrils the breath of*
> *life; and man became a living being* (Genesis 2:7).

As God-breathed creations, we carry His image upon us.
Because He is the author of His Word, it also bears His image.
When we carry God's Word into our prayers, we become partners with Him, equipped for every good work and able to breathe
life into our world.

THE WORD BECAME FLESH

Much of the world is acquainted with Jesus, the Son of
God who came to earth and lived in the flesh. But Jesus, the
second member of the Trinity, existed long before He appeared
on the earth. He has existed for all eternity, as the Gospel of
John indicates:

> *In the beginning was the Word, and the Word was*
> *with God, and the Word was God. He was in the*
> *beginning with God. All things were made through*
> *Him, and without Him nothing was made that was*
> *made. In Him was life, and the life was the light of*

men. And the light shines in the darkness, and the darkness did not comprehend it (John 1:1-5).

God's Word existed in the beginning of time. If we could see as far back as time goes, we would find that God's Word existed even before that.

The Word was working with God *and* the Word *was* God. But, how is that possible? The answer to this question is found in this divine truth: Jesus was in existence with God in the beginning—in the form of the Word.

How do we know that the "Word" spoken of in John 1:1-5 refers to Jesus? Consider the following Scriptures:

For there are three that bear witness in heaven: the Father, the Word, and the Holy Spirit; and these three are one (1 John 5:7).

He was clothed with a robe dipped in blood, and His name is called The Word of God (Revelation 19:13).

And the Word became flesh and dwelt among us, and we beheld His glory, the glory as of the only begotten of the Father, full of grace and truth (John 1:14).

Jesus was working with God in the beginning, and He was God. He had not yet taken on human form; He had not yet been born in Bethlehem. He had not yet died on the cross or been glorified as Christ. He was in the form of the Word.

The mystery of the Trinity is one of the greatest mysteries in the Bible. God the Father, God the Son, and God the Holy Spirit are all equal, yet they function in different ways on the earth.

In the creation of the world, all three members of the Godhead were present and active. The Bible is very specific regarding the role of the Word in all that occurred. Scripture tells us that *"all things were made through Him* [the Word]" (John 1:3). Hebrews 11:3 declares, *"...The worlds were framed by the word of God, so that the things which are seen were not made of things which are visible."*

How does this role in creation relate to the topic of prayer and its power source? Very simply: without the Word of God speaking things into existence, nothing would have been created. The earth would have remained *"without form and void,"* just as Genesis 1:2 describes its condition *"in the beginning."*

We can see why it is so important for us to use God's Word in our prayers today! God Himself used the Word in the creation of the world. We must follow His example and use the Word to bring about the "creation" of His plans here on earth.

All aspects of God's will are accomplished through His Word. The Word brings life and light to men. It is the light of the world and a light to our individual paths. The Word illuminates the darkness, brings clarity to confusion, and directs us in the ways we should go.

The Word equips us for life. We were never meant to live our lives in the darkness. In the darkness, our minds, our emotions—the

> **The Word brings life and light to all.**

elements of what we call the flesh—scream for relief. In the darkness, we operate out of our own will; we are preoccupied by the flesh and do not care about the things of God. From the perspective of the darkness, our flesh knows only that it will someday die, and so it seeks the pleasures of today for temporary satisfaction.

But we do not have to live in the darkness. We are called to be children of light, people of the Word!

In John 1, Word is actually translated from the Greek word *lógos*. The word *lógos* means "the divine expression" of God."[2]

The Logos, or Word, described in this passage is Jesus, and when you pray the Word over a certain situation, you are literally "applying Jesus" to that problem or circumstance.

On the other hand, when you don't use the Word in your prayers, no matter how sincere you may be, you are not actually applying Jesus to the situation.

Additionally, speaking the written Word (Scripture) allows the Living Word (Jesus Christ) to operate in the earth. When you speak God's Word, it is infused with power, and it begins to work to accomplish God's will.

Hear me on this: learn to use God's Word in your prayers so that Jesus, the One with all of the authority and power, can move in your life and produce God's plans for you.

When Jesus Himself taught about prayer, He warned against using meaningless words: *When you pray, do not use vain repetitions as the heathen do. For they think that they will be heard for their many words* (Matthew 6:7).

We must learn to make our words in prayer count! The length of our prayers means nothing if we are not praying the Word, praying effective prayers that will yield results.

THE PURPOSE OF THE WORD

> *All Scripture is given by inspiration of God, and is profitable for doctrine [or teaching], for reproof, for correction, for instruction in righteousness, that the man of God may be complete, thoroughly equipped for every good work* (2 Timothy 3:16-17).

There are many purposes for the Word of God: to teach, to reprove, to correct, to instruct, but all of these relate to the final result in the life of the believer: righteousness.

Whenever you are in doubt about what you should be doing, go to the Word. Whatever decisions you have to make, go to the Word and see what it has to say about the situations you are facing. The Word will distinguish between what is right and what is wrong.

Second Timothy 3:16 tells us that the Word is "profitable." The word *profitable* means "yielding advantageous returns or results."[3] When we pray the Word of God, we will see our prayers become effective; we will witness the advantageous results they yield. It is to our advantage to use the Word when we pray!

> **The Word distinguishes between right and wrong.**

If you want to see any sort of positive change in your life, you must use the Word of God. You can read self-help books if you like, but the basis for change in your life should be the Bible, not self-help books.

Reading Christian books, such as the one you are holding in your hands right now, can be very helpful. Books like this one encourage your faith and teach the ways of God. Yet, these books must always be considered supplements to the highest Book, the Word of God.

As Paul explained in his letter to Timothy, the Word is "profitable" in many ways. Let's focus on three:

- The Word *teaches* us. The word *teach* means "to impart knowledge of or skill in."[4] God's Word brings life as it imparts knowledge and gives us skills to operate in God's Kingdom.

- The Word *reproves* us. The word *reprove* means "to express disapproval of."[5] The Scriptures are the measuring stick by which we can judge our thoughts, attitudes, and behaviors. How can we know whether we are doing something wrong? Look in the Word. And how do we know whether we are doing something right? Again— look in the Word. It is the standard by which we must measure ourselves.

▪ The Word *trains us in righteousness.* The Bible instructs us in the ways of God, which are completely foreign to our human nature. Christians are called to live by a different set of rules from the one the world follows. The world says that it is perfectly fine to argue with your neighbors, even "cuss them out" if necessary, when they do something that angers you. But that is not a "perfectly fine" way for Christians to behave. The Scriptures say to "love your enemy" and "turn the other cheek." And that is what the Christian is called to do. How does a Christian learn to behave in godly ways? Simply by following the Word.

As we humble ourselves before the Lord and allow His Word to teach us, reprove us, correct us, and train us in righteousness, several things will begin to take place:

First, the condition of our hearts will be revealed. You may be completely unaware of an issue in your heart that God wants to address, but as you diligently meditate on His Word, go to Bible studies, go to church, and *pray* the Word, God will bring it to your attention. The Word will pinpoint the condition of your heart.

Second, our minds will be renewed. This process produces a spiritual chain reaction that leads to the fulfillment of God's will in our lives. Consider Paul's words:

And do not be conformed to this world, but be transformed by the renewing of your mind, that you may prove what is that good and acceptable and perfect will of God (Romans 12:2).

Before the Fall of humankind, the minds of Adam and Eve never needed to be renewed; they were not contending with a sin nature. But since that time, we must continually battle against the carnal mind. We must continue to go to church, study the Word, and spend time in prayer, or our minds will immediately begin to slip back into natural, worldly ways of thinking. The mind must constantly be renewed, and that can only take place through the Word of God.

Third, the Word helps us to understand who God is. Without the Scriptures, it would be difficult to get to know our heavenly Father, to learn of His greatness and power—and His love. But He has provided us with His Word, an account of

> *His Word makes Himself known to you.*

His dealings with humankind throughout the ages, a living testimony to His character, a way to make Himself known to us.

The Book of Psalms alone contains powerful teachings about who God is. The psalms speak of His works revealed in nature, His mighty acts of deliverance, and the history of His dealings with humanity. The psalms declare God's glory, majesty, greatness, and love for all of His creation.

Fourth, the Word is the one weapon that will keep the enemy under our feet.

Consider Jesus' response when the devil came to Him with temptation. Jesus simply said: *"It is written..."* (Matt. 4:4,7,10). Every time He was tempted, Jesus responded with these words, and satan could not gain a foothold.

Jesus provided this as a pattern for us to use to defeat the enemy in our own lives. We are to respond saying: *"It is written...."*

Jesus passed His authority on to His followers: *"I give you the authority to trample on serpents and scorpions, and over all the power of the enemy, and nothing shall by any means hurt you"* (Luke 10:19).

When we speak the Word in the authority of the name of Jesus, satan trembles! We defeat him with the Word of God.

THE POWER OF THE WORD

The Word of God is uniquely powerful; it is able to create what did not exist before, and it is mighty in bringing change to our circumstances.

> *For the Word of God is living and powerful, and sharper than any two-edged sword, piercing even to the division of soul and spirit, and of joints and marrow, and is a discerner of the thoughts and intents of the heart. And there is no creature hidden from His sight, but all things are naked and open to the eyes of Him to whom we must give account* (Hebrews 4:12-13).

This passage of Scripture brilliantly describes the dynamism of the Word. It reminds us that the Word was given with a purpose—to bring forth God's will in every life and in every situation.

The Word of God is alive. "The Word of God is living." In the same way that prayer is a living entity, the Word of God is alive unto itself.

As we learned from John 1, the Word *is* God; it is Jesus in Word form. As long as God is alive and seated on His throne, Jesus is alive. And if Jesus is alive, the Word of God is alive. Because it is alive and has a being and a distinct existence, it is capable of causing things to happen, of creating change upon the earth. God is purposeful regarding His Word: *"He sends out His command to the earth; His word runs very swiftly"* (Ps. 147:15).

The Word of God is powerful. *"The Word of God is living and powerful."* God's Word is "energetically efficacious"! It has the ability to act or perform with effectiveness—it gets things done! It is a force, a cause of motion unto itself.

The power of God's Word can be most easily seen in the creation of the world. In Genesis 1, we read words like this: *"Then God said, 'Let there be...'; and there was..."* (see verses 3-24). Whatever God said *happened.*

Hebrews 11:3 declares: *"By faith we understand that the worlds were framed by the word of God, so that the things which are seen were not made of things which are visible."* We have been given the same authority in the earth, to speak forth God's Word and see results. God has invested a great deal in our ability as humans to speak. His Word says: *"Death and life are in the power of the tongue, and those who love it will eat its fruit"* (Prov. 18:21).

The Word of God is a sharp weapon. *"The Word of God is... sharper than any two-edged sword."* The Word of God is the sword that we use to defeat the enemy. It is the weapon we use to recapture everything the devil has stolen from our lives and the lives of our family members and loved ones.

The Word can be used defensively to keep the enemy at bay. But it can also be used as an offensive weapon to destroy the enemy's plans. When we pray God's Word, it produces what God wants for us.

The Word of God separates the soul and the spirit. *"The Word of God is...sharper than any two-edged sword, piercing even to the division of soul and spirit, and of joints and marrow."* The Word will separate the carnal man (the flesh, the soul) from the spiritual man.

The Greek word for "soul" that is used here is *psuche* (psookhay'),[6] and it literally means "the seat of the feelings, of desire, of the affections and of aversions."[7] The *soul* contains all of our fleshly desires, affections, and emotions—the things that our hearts crave when we are not in full submission to the Lord.

In contrast, the Greek word for "spirit" is *pneuma* (pnyoo'-mah),[8] which refers to that part of man that is receptive to the Spirit of God. The Word of God is the only thing that can discern, separate, or distinguish between the carnal person and the spiritual person.

The Word of God discerns our thoughts and intentions. "The Word of God is...a discerner of the thoughts and intents of the heart." The Word of God is capable of judging the deepest parts of our hearts. It can discern what is going on inside a person; it is able to reveal what a person's true motives, intents, and thoughts are—even the ones they would never share with anyone else.

Put this principle to the test. If you are experiencing difficulty at your place of employment (or in your home, business, church, etc.), begin to pray the Word in that place. Go there before other people arrive or stay late after everyone has left. Speak the Word aloud in your office, home, or church. Allow the Word time to do its work of discerning the thoughts and intents of people's hearts. Watch and see what is revealed. The truth always comes out when God's Word is spoken.

The Word of God is truth. "All things are naked and open to the eyes of Him to whom we must give account." God's Word is Truth. The Greek word for "truth" is aletheia[9] which means "what is true in any matter under consideration."[10] The word true indicates, "the state of being the case of the fact."[11] Jesus prayed that we would be sanctified by God's Word, which is Truth:

> *But now I come to You, and these things I speak in the world, that they may have My joy fulfilled in themselves. I have given them Your word; and the world has hated them because they are not of the world, just*

as I am not of the world. I do not pray that You should take them out of the world, but that You should keep them from the evil one. They are not of the world, just as I am not of the world. Sanctify them by Your truth. Your word is truth. As You sent Me into the world, I also have sent them into the world (John 17:13-18).

To be sanctified by Truth is to become more and more Christlike and better equipped to go into the world and do God's bidding. Earlier we considered the process of sanctification from the specific perspective of renewing the mind:

I [also] *beseech you, therefore, brethren, by the mercies of God, that you present your bodies a living sacrifice, holy, acceptable to God, which is your reasonable service. And do not be conformed to this world, but be transformed by the renewing of your mind, that you may prove what is that good and acceptable and perfect will of God* (Romans 12:1-2).

The hope found in this passage from Romans is that we would be reshaped by Truth, that our minds and our prayers would be so filled with God's Word that we would be completely transformed. When that occurs, our prayers will yield amazing results for the Kingdom of God!

THE WORD'S JOB DESCRIPTION

Just as NASA's mission is accomplished through the combined work of astronauts who perform different job descriptions, God's will is carried out through His Word, which also has multiple "job functions." Those functions are set in motion every time we load His Word into our prayers. When working in combination, these functions are able to complete the necessary work to accomplish God's mission(s) for our lives.

The Word's multiple job functions include:

1. A Navigation System:

The Word of God directs and guides our prayers to the plans of God in the supernatural and brings them back to the earth. It also guides our lives in accordance with God's will and gives us direction. The Bible says: *"Your Word is a lamp to my feet and a light to my path"* (Ps. 119:105).

2. An Irrigation System:

The Word of God waters the seeds that have been sown in the form of Word-filled prayers and brings forth the intended fruit. It provides the necessary moisture for life and growth. When Ezekiel spoke God's Word to the dry bones in Ezekiel 37, his spoken word watered the bones and they began to live again.

The Bible describes the heavenly "irrigation process" this way:

> *For as the rain comes down, and the snow from heaven, and do not return there, but water the earth, and make it bring forth and bud, that it may give seed to the sower and bread to the eater, so shall my word be that goes forth from My mouth; it shall not return to Me void, but it shall accomplish what I please, and it shall prosper in the thing for which I sent it* (Isaiah 55:10-11).

3. A Support System:

The Word of God provides the support necessary to build an effective prayer.

The world that we live in is framed by God's Word. This frame can be likened to the frame of a house. When a house is being built, a frame must be erected to give the house shape. The frame defines the shape of the house and supports the necessary components of the house. Without the frame, there can be no house. Sheetrock is laid on the frame, electrical wiring is laced through the frame, and plumbing is placed within the frame. The critical elements for building a house are supported by the frame.

God's Word is the key support for our existence. Every important element of life hangs on His Word. A prayer unframed by the Word of God does not yield results. Here's what the Word says about itself:

> *By faith we understand that the worlds were framed by the word of God, so that the things which are seen were not made of things which are visible* (Hebrews 11:3).

4. *A Manufacturing System:*

The Word of God makes on earth what God has created in Heaven. When we speak His Word, it begins to construct the earthly manifestation of God's plans for our lives. Anything we experience on earth that reflects His Kingdom has already been formulated in Heaven. Praying God's Word connects us with His reality and makes His reality ours. The creation demonstrates this dynamic: *"Then God said, 'Let there be light'; and there was light"* (Gen. 1:3)

5. *A Healing Agent:*

The Word of God is medicine for our souls and our bodies. When we are sick, we are to speak life into the sickness using His Word. It is true that God will use doctors to bring about healing, but God's Word is what brings the cure. The Bible is clear on this:

> [God] *sent His Word and healed them, and delivered them from their destructions* (Psalm 107:20).

My son, give attention to My words; incline your ear to My sayings. Do not let them depart from your eyes; keep them in the midst of your heart; for they are life to those who find them, and health to all their flesh (Proverbs 4:20-22).

6. *Food for Living:*

The Word of God is the nourishment that keeps us alive and healthy. Natural food alone will not sustain the believer. without the spiritual nutrition of God's Word, we will die a slow death. Jesus said as much: *"It is written, 'Man shall not live by bread alone, but by every word that proceeds from the mouth of God'"* (Matt. 4:4).

7. *A Surgical Tool:*

The Word of God is a double-edged sword that has the power to divide the soul from the spirit. It is able to remove or repair anything that prevents us from being perfected to do His will. The following passage bears repeating:

The Word of God is living and powerful, and sharper than any two-edged sword, piercing even to the division of soul and spirit, and of joints and marrow, and is a discerner of the thoughts and intents of the heart (Hebrews 4:12).

8. *A Weapon:*

The Word of God enables us to stand toe-to-toe with the devil and prevail against him. In Matthew 4:1-11, Jesus showed us how to foil the plans of the devil by using God's Word so that the Master's plan succeeds. Though tempted three times by satan, Jesus used the might of the Word to remain steadfast and to cause the tempter to flee:

[Jesus] *answered and said, "It is written:' Man shall not live by bread alone, but by every word that proceeds from the mouth of God'"* (verse 4).

Jesus said to him, "It is written again, 'You shall not tempt the Lord your God'" (verse 7).

Jesus said to him, "Away with you, satan! For it is written, 'You shall worship the Lord your God, and Him only you shall serve'" (verse 10).

The authority Jesus had is the authority we have—to use the Word of God. When we do, the devil will flee from us, his actions will be destroyed, and God's plans will succeed.

It is only when we pray, using God's Word, that we can truly say, "Mission accomplished!" The Bible makes this enduring promise:

So shall My word be that goes forth from My mouth; it shall not return to Me void, but it shall accomplish what I please, and it shall prosper in the thing for which I sent it (Isaiah 55:11).

PRACTICE PRAYING THE WORD

Before we move on in our study of prayer, this is an excellent time for you to begin to practice praying God's Word.

Below are scriptural prayer examples and exercises. The examples demonstrate how you can personalize Scriptures and pray them directly to God. The exercises are your opportunity to do the personalizing yourself.

As you read the following Scripture passages and prayers, notice how the prayers have been reworded to position you as the pray-er engaged in Word-based conversation with God.

After you have completed Exercises 1 and 2, you will be ready to open your Bible, choose a passage (the Book of Psalms is a good place to start), personalize it, and pray it back to God. (See Exercise 3.)

Make this a practice in your daily life—especially in conjunction with the principles found throughout this book. You will begin to experience more power in your prayer life and you will see better results!

EXAMPLE 1:
PRAYER OF PRAISE (from Psalm 97:1-6)

The following Scripture passage contains expressions of praise to God.

Scripture Passage

> *The Lord reigns; let the earth rejoice; let the multitude of isles be glad! Clouds and darkness surround Him; righteousness and justice are the foundation of His throne. A fire goes before Him, and burns up His enemies round about. His lightnings light the world; the earth sees and trembles. The mountains melt like wax at the presence of the Lord, at the presence of the Lord of the whole earth. The heavens declare His righteousness, and all the peoples see His glory.*

Scriptural Prayer

> *Father, You reign; let the earth rejoice; let the multitude of the isles be glad! Clouds and darkness surround You; righteousness and justice are the foundations of Your throne. A fire goes before You, and burns up Your enemies round about. Your lightnings light the world; the earth sees and trembles. The mountains melt like wax at Your presence; at Your presence, the Lord of the whole earth. The heavens declare Your righteousness and all the peoples see Your glory. Amen.*

EXERCISE 1:
PRAYER OF PRAISE
(from Psalm 95:1-5)

Read the following Scripture passage. Then proceed to the scriptural prayer and fill in the blanks to personalize it. (The first two blanks have been filled in for you.)

Scripture Passage

> *Oh come, let us sing to the Lord! Let us shout joyfully to the Rock of our salvation. Let us come before His presence with thanksgiving; let us shout joyfully to Him with psalms. For the Lord is the great God, and the great King above all gods. In His hand are the deep places of the earth; the heights of the hills are His also. The sea is His, for He made it; and His hands formed the dry land.*

Scriptural Prayer

> *Today I come to sing to You, Lord! _____ shout joyfully to the Rock of _____ salvation. _____ come before _____ presence with thanksgiving; ____ shout joyfully to _____ with psalms. For_____ are the great God and the great King above all gods. In _____ hand are the deep places of the earth; the heights of the hills are _____ also. The sea is _____, for _____ made it; and _____hands formed the dry land.*

(See Appendix A in *The Power Source* for the completed version of this prayer.)

EXAMPLE 2:
PRAYER OF BLESSING FOR THOSE WHO FEAR THE LORD (from Psalm 128)

The following Scripture passage contains promiss of God for you and your loved ones.

Scripture Passage

Blessed is every one who fears the Lord, who walks in His ways. When you eat the labor of your hands, you shall be happy, and it shall be well with you. Your wife shall be like a fruitful vine in the very heart of your house, your children like olive plants all around your table. Behold, thus shall the man be blessed who fears the Lord. The Lord bless you out of Zion, and may you see the good of Jerusalem all the days of your life. Yes, may you see your children's children. Peace be upon Israel.

Scriptural Prayer

Father, I am blessed because I fear You and walk in Your ways. When I eat the labor of my hands, I shall be happy, and it shall be well with me. My spouse shall be like a fruitful vine in the very heart of my house, my children like olive plants all around my table. Behold, I shall be blessed because I fear You, Lord. Lord, bless me out of Zion, and I will see the good of Jerusalem all the days of my life. Yes, I will see my children's children. Peace be upon Israel. Amen.

EXERCISE 2:
BIBLICAL CONFESSION ABOUT THE BELIEVER (from Psalm 92:12-15)

Read the following Scripture passage. Then proceed to the scriptural prayer and fill in the blanks to personalize it.

Scripture Passage

> *The righteous shall flourish like a palm tree, he shall grow like a cedar in Lebanon. Those who are planted in the house of the Lord shall flourish in the courts of our God. They shall still bear fruit in old age; they shall be fresh and flourishing, to declare that the Lord is upright; He is my rock, and there is no unrighteousness in Him.*

Scriptural Prayer

As the righteous, _____ shall flourish like a palm tree. _____ shall grow like a cedar in Lebanon. _____ _____ planted in the house of the Lord, and _____ shall flourish in the courts of _____ God. _____ shall bear fruit in_____ old age; _____ shall be fresh (fat) and flourishing (green), and _____ _____ declare that the Lord is upright; _____ _____ my rock, and there is no unrighteousness in _____.

(See Appendix A in The Power Source for the completed version of this prayer.)

EXERCISE 3:
DECLARATION OF GOD'S WILL FOR SUCCESSFUL LIVING (from Psalm 1)

Now, try praying God's Word straight from your Bible. Read Psalm 1 and personalize it so that it becomes a prayer from you or a prayer for a loved one. If necessary, write out the Scripture and plug yourself into it. Pray this Scripture over your life, expecting it to accomplish God's promises for you.

After writing your scriptural prayer, compare it to the example provided in Appendix A. Please note that it is OK to articulate Scripture slightly differently from the way it is written in the Bible. It is usually necessary to change the wording somewhat in order to plug yourself into the scriptural prayer.

For example, Psalm 92:12-15 begins: *"The righteous shall flourish like a palm tree...."* Your scriptural prayer using this psalm begins, "As the righteous, I shall flourish like a palm tree." Psalm 95:1-5 starts out with *"Oh come, let us sing to the Lord!"* The scriptural prayer using this psalm starts out with "Today I come to sing to You, Lord!"

Personalize the Scripture to include yourself, but do not add, delete, or alter words that would change the context or meaning of the Scripture. I recommend that you use a Bible version that closely communicates the original meaning of Scripture. The examples and exercises in this chapter are based on the New King James Version of the Bible. However, the New Living Translation is another great version to use because it is written in contemporary language and reads closer to the way we express ourselves today.

About Suzette Caldwell

With an intense determination to implement God's purpose for her life, Pastor Suzette Caldwell has studied and taught prayer for 17 years. She is Associate Pastor for Windsor Village United Methodist Church and Board Chairman for the Kingdom Builders Prayer Institute. Suzette is married to Pastor Kirbyjon H. Caldwell. They have three children.

ENDNOTES

1. James Strong, *The New Strong's Exhaustive Concordance of the Bible* (Nashville: Thomas Nelson Publishers, 1995), s.v. "theópneustos" (#2315).

2. James Strong, s.v. "lógos" (#3056).

3. *Merriam-Webster's Collegiate Dictionary*, 10th ed., s.v. "profitable."

4. *Webster's New Universal Unabridged Dictionary*, 1994, s.v. "teach."

5. Ibid., s.v. "reprove."

6. James Strong, s.v. "psuche" (#5590).

7. BibleWorks 7, CD-ROM, version 7, BibleWorks.

8. James Strong, s.v. "pneuma" (#4151).

9. James Strong, s.v. "aletheia" (#0225).

10. BibleWorks 7, CD-ROM, version 7, BibleWorks.

11. *Merriam-Webster's Collegiate Dictionary*, 10th ed., s.v. "true."

Chapter 7

PRAYING IN ANOTHER DIMENSION

by Sue Curran

*So continuing daily with one accord in the
temple, and breaking bread from house
to house, they ate their food with gladness
and simplicity of heart* (Acts 2:46).

In the nations where God is moving mightily, it is normal for
believers to be involved in continual prayer, corporately and
individually. You can go to their sanctuaries at any hour of the
day or night and find believers praying. Their churches have truly
become what Jesus ordained them to be: "a house of prayer for

all nations." They have embraced the biblical pattern of prayer, which has unlocked the power of God into their lives. And their hearts have truly become temples of God, committed to a life-style of prayer.

COMMITMENT TO PRAYER

Do you realize that the nation of Israel was accustomed to praying three times a day as their regular prayer lifestyle? Daniel prayed three times a day. The psalmist David declared: *"Evening and morning and at noon I will pray, and cry aloud, and He shall hear my voice. He has redeemed my soul in peace from the battle that was against me"* (Ps. 55:17-18a). And fire came down from Heaven when Elijah prayed at the evening hour of prayer.

This biblical pattern of daily prayer was maintained in the lives of the early Church. We read in the Book of Acts that Peter and John were going to the temple at the hour of prayer when they healed the lame man at the Gate Beautiful. It was the first hour of prayer when the Holy Spirit fell on the day of Pentecost. And it was the hour of prayer when Peter went up to the rooftop to pray and had his revelation to take the good news to the Gentiles. In the Book of Acts we read that the Church gathered daily in prayer: *"So continuing daily with one accord in the temple, and breaking bread from house to house, they ate their food with gladness and simplicity of heart"* (Acts 2:46).

Even today, practicing Jews pray three times a day, and Muslims respond to a call to prayer five times a day. While ministering in India, I was awakened at 5:30 A.M. by the Muslim call to prayer. To this day I can hear the haunting, mournful cry of that call, to

> *When he prayed to Jesus, he was keenly aware that Someone was there, listening.*

which an entire population responds, halting all activity to pray to their god.

One former Muslim testified that he had prayed over 5,600 hours to Allah. When He found Jesus as His true Savior, he rejoiced at the great difference his personal relationship with Christ made in prayer. When he prayed to Jesus, he was keenly aware that Someone was there, listening. Yet, even in his religious darkness, he had been committed to prayer to fulfill his obligation to Allah. As a Christian, this established prayer commitment could now serve him well, as he learned to enter into the presence of the living God through prayer.

OLD TESTAMENT PATTERN

God promised Old Testament saints: *"Call to Me, and I will answer you, and show you great and mighty things, which you do not know"* (Jer. 33:3). The word *call* translated here is the Hebrew word *qará*, which implies "accosting a person, crying out to them, properly calling them by name" (Strong's #7121). It involves perseverance, determination, commitment, and inner tenacity. Such fervent prayer brings revelation of God's will into specific situations that can only be changed through prayer.

> *Today, nations are being influenced by the power of prophetic prayer.*

History records the exploits of great men and women of prayer. Queen Victoria of England, in the pomp and power of her reign declared: "I fear nothing except the prayers of John Knox." The Englishman, Reese Howells, a mighty intercessor, prayed earnestly during World War II for his nation. He announced that the Germans would not invade England. However, when they began their invasion, Howells went back to God in fervent prayer. It was then that Hitler aborted his planned invasion of England, sending the troops to Russia instead.

Today, nations are being influenced as well by the power of prophetic prayer and declaration. Archbishop Duncan-Williams prophesied that a certain general would be elected the next president of Nigeria. Many found it hard to believe him because that general had already been president 20 years earlier. However, it happened as he had prophesied it would. The nation elected this veteran general again to be president of Nigeria. God reveals His plans to those who intercede for His will in the nations.

NEW TESTAMENT PATTERN

The Book of the Acts of the Apostles reveals a deep commitment of the early Church to a lifestyle of fervent prayer. The apostles established their lives on prayer and the reading of the Word, delegating the serving of tables to other good men, full of the Holy Spirit and wisdom (see Acts 6). Stephen, one of those servers, who also did great wonders and signs among the people (see Acts 6:8), prayed for his murderers when they stoned him to death, making him a martyr for the gospel. These early Christians prayed for their enemies, for protection, for boldness, for deliverance; they prayed together and when they were alone. They prayed consistently, several times a day.

Christians who do great things and have great power with God are people who are deeply committed to prayer. Dr. Yonggi Cho sets aside three times a day for prayer. Before ministering in the pulpit, he prays for three hours. When ministering in Japan, he prays for six hours before preaching. He has established a place called "Prayer Mountain, where people go to stay in tiny grottoes alone for days and weeks at time to pray and fast. There are 25,000 people praying there every day, and this has been continuing for over 20 years. Again, Duncan-Williams admonishes believers:

> If you want to see the miracles of God, commit yourself to prayer like crazy. Make prayer a lifestyle. Commit to it until you die. The reason we don't have miracles in the church today is that we don't pray. Take it up to another level. Apply more pressure to the enemy. Make up your mind to "push" to birth the purposes of God. When you feel the pain of travail, don't stop praying.[1]

My friend, Bishop Bart Pierce pastors Rock City Church in Baltimore, Maryland.[2] He made this general comparison from what he observed among the Africans: "They do not sit when they pray; they stand. They walk, they get loud, they pray with fervor. In contrast, my observation of American Christians in prayer meetings is that they want to sit, be quiet, and not use energy or show strong emotion."

> *If you want to see the miracles of God, commit yourself to prayer like crazy.*
> —DUNCAN-WILLIAMS

As American Christians, we desperately need a paradigm shift concerning our commitment to prayer. The church's biblical purpose for existing is to become a house of prayer. Therefore, every believer must make a commitment to fulfill that purpose. Otherwise, the church will not be a dwelling place for the presence and power of God we so desperately need. Souls cannot be saved without that divine power. Personal destiny cannot be realized without it. Neither can the enemy of our souls be vanquished without the supernatural power of God.

BIBLICAL PRAYER PATTERNS

Until I began to teach American believers regarding prayer in another dimension, I personally did not realize how committed we are to our traditional attitudes. We are opposed to changing even our postures and approaches to prayer, many of which are not biblical. Bart Pierce concluded that in America too often we have allowed *religious* people to establish the environment for our prayer ministry. Religious tradition is one step away from reality, preferring form and familiarity to fervor and function. While our traditions allow us a feeling of religious satisfaction, they fall short of bringing effective results in the lives and situations of hurting people.

When Bart Pierce ministered at our church, one of our more astute members made this observation concerning his manner of praying: "I don't think I have ever seen anyone pray as fervently, without ceasing, as Pastor Pierce did during our pre-service prayer. His intense focus was impressive." According to Pierce, there are at least five specific characteristics of the kind of prayer Africans engage in that makes their lives and churches so powerful. He observed the following elements in the prayers of the Africans that help them pray in another dimension:

1. Their prayers are *vocal*, rather than silent.

2. They pray *fervently*, focused on specific needs.

3. They consistently pray the Word—*through proclamation*.

4. Their entire focus is *vertical*, addressing God alone.

5. Their prayers are full of the authority of a *prophetic* anointing.[3]

I began to study the biblical foundation for each of these characteristics of prayer—vocal, fervent, proclaiming the Word, vertical, prophetic—that characterize the powerful prayer lives of believers in other nations. As I did, what became very clear, by contrast, was the lack of energy, focus, authority, and prophetic anointing that characterizes much of the praying in our American churches. If we learn to yield our hearts and minds (our old wineskins) to biblical patterns of prayer, we can begin to see the power of God released in our churches and our nation, just as these precious Christians in other nations have experienced. The prayer lives of Christians in these revival nations closely resemble the fervency of the Old Testament prophets as well as the New Testament Church.

Our church is on a quest to establish ourselves in the kind of powerful prayer life we are observing in other nations. We want to see the same proportions of harvest of souls, the kinds of healing and multiplied miracles, even to the raising of the dead, as God is doing in these revival nations. It is time for American churches to take a quantum leap into prayer in another dimension. We need to learn to use prayer as a weapon against the onslaught of the enemy, who continues to "steal, kill, and destroy" (see John 10:10). He continually attacks the spiritual lives and integrity of our families, our churches, and our nation. We must insist on the victory of Calvary and bring the Kingdom of God to earth through powerful, persistent prayer.

FIVE SMOOTH STONES

Until we grasp the fact that the essence of true prayer is *spiritual* and must be accomplished through the Holy Spirit working effectively in our spiritual life, we will not enter into another dimension of prayer. We have to lay aside intellectual prayers, based on facts and knowledge. Analyzing situations and explaining them to God is a futile attempt to pray. God's perspective of life is much different from ours. We cannot pray effectively if we are filled with strife and complaint or other negative emotional responses. We must learn to abandon ourselves in complete trust and confidence in God, who has given us the recourse of prayer to present our petitions in faith to Him.

Jesus made it very clear to His disciples that He wanted them to *ask*, to *seek*, and to *knock*, to receive answers to prayer (see Luke 11:9). He declared: *"And in that day you will ask Me nothing. Most assuredly, I say to you, whatever you ask the Father in My name He will give you. Until now you have asked nothing in My name. Ask, and you will receive, that your joy may be full"* (John 16:23-24).

> **It is time for American churches to take a quantum leap into prayer in another dimension.**

My dear friend, Dr. Fuchsia Pickett, shared with me on one occasion a spiritual vision God gave her in which He taught her how to use spiritual weapons of warfare. She was an avid student of the Word of God, as a Methodist professor, before she was miraculously healed from her deathbed and baptized with the Holy Spirit. She had not believed in either the reality of healing for the Church today or Holy Spirit baptism—until she received both on the same morning. Then God began to teach her His ways, as she yielded her strong intellect as well as her theological degrees to Him. She learned to approach God in the simplicity of a child. Dr. Pickett recorded this vision in her book, *Stones of Remembrance*,[4] which I have summarized here:

> I was praying before I went to bed and the Lord spoke to me, "If you will spend the night with Me, as the

day dawns I will teach you how to have power over the devil." ...Just as the dawn came, I fell into a trance and began to see a young man with broad shoulders and a ruddy face. He had a shepherd's sling draped over his shoulder. As I looked at him, I said, "You are David." Then I began to watch a drama unfold. As David reached into the brook at his feet and picked up five stones, I saw a huge person walk into the other side of the room. I looked up, startled by his size, and whispered, "You are Goliath." Then I saw David put four stones away and sling one stone at the giant. The Holy Spirit asked me, "In what authority did he sling that rock?" I remembered David's words to Goliath: "...but I come to you in the name of the Lord of Hosts" (1 Sam. 17:45).

I watched in the vision as Goliath fell when David's smooth stone found its mark in his forehead. Then I became a part of the vision, as the Holy Spirit said, "Now, you take the other four stones and place them in your sling." Now I had to use these stones to defeat the enemy. First, the Holy Spirit asked me, "What stone did Jesus throw at the devil?" I answered, "Jesus' response to the devil was 'It is written.'" Then I hurled the stone of the Word at the enemy. Then the Spirit asked me, "What is the line the enemy cannot cross?" I responded, "The blood of Jesus. That is what the Passover was all about." And I hurled the second stone. Then I heard the question, "What is the source of your strength for battle?" I responded, "It is 'not by might, nor by power, but by My spirit, saith the Lord of hosts'" (Zech. 4:6 KJV). I understood that this stone represented the power of the Holy Spirit.

Finally, the Holy Spirit asked, "Whose faith is it?" And I responded with the words of Paul, "The life which I now live in the flesh I live by the faith of the Son of God" (Gal. 2:20 KJV). I understood that defeating the enemy is not about standing and yelling and stomping our feet. It involves using the divine arsenal of weapons God has given us—the name of the Lord, His Word, His blood, the power of His Spirit, and His faith. Then the Holy Spirit instructed me, "Put those five smooth stones in the sling of praise and go conquer the enemy."

In this dramatic vision, God taught Fuchsia Pickett more about prayer and defeating the enemy of our souls than she had learned from her theological studies. Too often we have based our prayers on our ideas, our complaints, or our religious phrases to try to defeat the devil. Satan is not afraid of our religious formulas, our own thoughts, or our intellectual challenges. We must learn to use the effective spiritual weapons against him that God has given to us.

The *Word* of God washes us, sanctifies us, and renews our minds (see John 17:17; Rom. 12:1-2). The *blood* of Christ saves us from our sin and provides healing for us (see 1 Pet. 2:24; 1 John 1:7). When we are praying against principalities and powers in spiritual warfare with the enemy, we need to declare our covering in the blood of Jesus in that moment. We are doing very real battle against spirits without bodies and *"spiritual wickedness in high places"* (Eph. 6:12 KJV).

The Scriptures teach that *faith* is a gift of God (see Eph. 2:8) and that it comes by hearing the Word of God (see Rom. 10:17). The apostle Paul declared: *"The life which I now live in the flesh I live by the faith of the Son of God, who loved me and gave Himself for me"* (Gal. 2:20b). And John declared, *"This is the victory that overcometh the world, even our faith"* (1 John 5:4b KJV). We need to learn to use this mighty weapon of faith and ask God to increase it.

We are also admonished in the Scriptures to be filled with the *Spirit* and to walk in the Spirit: *"I say then: Walk in the Spirit, and you shall not fulfill the lust of the flesh"* (Gal. 5:16). And Jesus taught us to ask in His *name* in order to receive what we need (see John 16:23-24).

As we allow our old wineskins to be renewed by the Word of God, we will learn to effectively use these spiritual weapons God has given us to defeat the enemy of our souls: His Word, His blood, His faith, His Spirit, and His name. Their supernatural power, when released through fervent prayer, will give to us the victory over the enemy of our souls that we so desperately need.

About Sue Curran

Sue Curran and her husband, John, are cofounders and pastors of Shekinah Church in Blountville, Tennessee. Dr. Curran earned a Master's and Doctor of Divinity degree from Christian Life School of Theology, and is an adjunct professor for Beacon Institute of Ministry.

She is the author of several books, and her ministry extends to all continents and crosses many cultural and ethnic boundaries.

ENDNOTES

1. Archbishop Nicholas Duncan-Williams, www .actionworshipcenter.org.

2. Bishop Bart Pierce, Pastor, Rock City Church, Baltimore, MD., http://www.rockcitychurch.com.

3. Ibid.

4. Fuchsia Pickett, *Stones of Remembrance* (Lake Mary, FL: Charisma House, 1998), 76-77.

Chapter 8

THE LIFE-CHANGING BENEFITS OF FASTING

by Mahesh Chavda

"Now, therefore," says the Lord, "turn to Me with all your heart, with fasting, with weeping, and with mourning" (Joel 2:12).

Nearly every Christian I have talked with has had some questions and misconceptions about fasting. I think it is safe to say that fasting is one of the most misunderstood subjects in the Bible. That is sad when you begin to discover the incredible benefits you receive through fasting according to God's Word. There are 12 specific benefits of the "fast that God has chosen" listed in the Book of Isaiah:

Is this not the fast that I have chosen: to loose the bonds of wickedness, to undo the heavy burdens, to let the oppressed go free, and that you break every yoke?

Is it not to share your bread with the hungry, and that you bring to your house the poor who are cast out; when you see the naked, that you cover him, and not hide yourself from your own flesh?

Then your light shall break forth like the morning, your healing shall spring forth speedily, and your righteousness shall go before you; the glory of the Lord shall be your rear guard.

Then you shall call, and the Lord will answer; you shall cry, and He will say, "Here I am." If you take away the yoke from your midst, the pointing of the finger, and speaking wickedness,

If you extend your soul to the hungry and satisfy the afflicted soul, then your light shall dawn in the darkness, and your darkness shall be as the noonday.

The Lord will guide you continually, and satisfy your soul in drought, and strengthen your bones; you shall be like a watered garden, and like a spring of water, whose waters do not fail.

Those from among you shall build the old waste places; you shall raise up the foundations of many generations; and you shall be called the Repairer of the Breach, the Restorer of Streets to Dwell In (Isaiah 58:6-12).

Isaiah 58 is one of the best chapters in the Bible on the subject of fasting. I could stay on this passage for several chapters or an entire book! It is wonderful. There are at least 12 specific benefits of "the fast that God has chosen" in this passage:

1. Revelation

2. Healing and wholeness

3. Righteousness

4. The presence of the *shekinah* glory of God

5. Answered prayers

6. Continual guidance

7. Contentment

8. Refreshing

9. Strength

10. Work that endures (like an ever-flowing spring)

11. Raising up of future generations

12. Restoration

How does fasting *really* work? I don't know all the answers because this is one of God's great mysteries, but I can share what I've learned up to this point. For one thing, demons get very uncomfortable when Christians begin fasting. We know from the Scriptures that many of the diseases, ailments, mental problems, and chronic behavioral problems afflicting mankind are instigated or perpetuated by demonic forces who want to hinder God's people and generally torment God's highest creation.

I often recommend to people who are seeking a healing from the Lord that they fast before they come to our healing services.

Those who heed this advice often receive a supernatural healing from the Lord very quickly. I tell people, "If your loved one comes to services, have them fast beforehand. Ask them to drink fruit or vegetable juices, or to get by on salad." The observation of some kind of fast is important because it shows a desperation and determination to "touch the Lord," who alone is the Source of all healing. Demons cannot stay around too long when a person fasts, because fasting unto God creates a totally different atmosphere that welcomes the holy and repels the unholy. That is why demonic spirits get very uncomfortable around a person who fasts.

Any pastor or minister who is in a healing and deliverance ministry of any kind should make fasting part of his regular lifestyle. It is the spiritual equivalent of an athlete working out at the gym. As you fast and seek God's face, He will begin to plant an authority in you born out of intimacy with Him that the demons will recognize and fear.

> *Demonic spirits get very uncomfortable around a person who fasts.*

I remember receiving a phone call in 1973 from two pastors who said, "Brother Mahesh, we were praying for a man who is a homosexual and suddenly a demon began talking through him! We are afraid." I said, "Well, just cast the demon out of him," but again they told me that they were afraid. "But you are pastors," I said. The men persisted, saying, "Please, come help us," and finally I agreed to go.

I drove to their location and opened the front door to the house and found them hiding in the broom closet! When I said, "What are you doing here?" they motioned toward another part of the house and said, *"He's out there."*

I had been fasting, and I went into the room where this man was waiting. The man had been a homosexual for 18 years, and when I entered the room, he was standing there as if waiting for a chance to intimidate again. I could see that the demon had come to the surface. He was literally staring out of the man. I could see it because the man's whole countenance had been transformed into a mask of evil. He saw me and said in an incredibly evil tone, "Oh, *another man*. Come in, I'd like to have fellowship with you."

Now it was my turn to do the talking by the power of the Holy Spirit.

"You want to have fellowship with me? Do you know what the Scriptures say? '...if we walk in the light as He is in the light, we have *fellowship* with one another, and the *blood of Jesus Christ* cleanses us from all sin.' (See 1 John 1:7.)

"Now demon, can you say, 'The blood of Jesus'? [The thing could only growl at this point. The cocky tone disappeared instantly.] Demon, say 'the blood of Jesus' now! Come on!"

> *Now it was my turn to do the talking by the power of the Holy Spirit.*

The man's hands started twisting, and I could literally hear bones cracking. Then the man's ankles began to twist in a contorted manner, and he fell on the floor and started writhing. I said, "Stop doing that. Say, 'The blood of Jesus.' Say it now!" Finally he said, "The bl—, the bl—." Then the man seemed to regurgitate, and the demon came out screaming.

I returned to that area five years later, and a man knocked on my hotel door. I remembered his face, but the last time I had seen the man, he was lying on the floor while two ministers huddled in a broom closet in another room. This time, he said, "Brother Chavda, I want to introduce you to someone." He stepped aside so I could see the young lady who was with him and he said, "We have been married for five years, and I want you to know that when you prayed for me that day, *I was totally delivered*. Now I'm married and have normal desires."

Praise God! He is the great Deliverer.

Another time I was ministering in the morning service of a church in a university town in the Southwest. I had just come through a season of fasting and prayer, and the services were going very well in the large church building. The altar was so large that it could accommodate hundreds of people at once, and I felt like the Lord wanted to bless the *whole audience* at once, so I brought them all up to the altar. As the Lord anointed the people, many were falling or responding to God's presence in different ways.

Right in the middle of the altar service, the Spirit of God prompted me to say, "The Lord tells me there are twelve homosexuals and lesbians here. If you'll raise your hands and repent right now, the Lord will deliver each one of you."

Twelve hands went up instantly. Eight of the people were lesbians, and when they raised their hands it looked like they were suddenly dropped to the floor by a blow from a large hammer! I knew the Lord wanted to do more, so I went down to where they lay on the carpet. I didn't know much about lesbians. I thought they all had men's haircuts and wore jeans and bossed everybody around. One particular young woman had confessed that she was a lesbian, but she defied the usual stereotype. She was a beautiful, 21-year-old, blonde-haired young woman, but when I looked at her, her entire visage turned dark.

I told her, "You are being delivered from a demon of death. In fact, it is a spirit of suicide. You tried to commit suicide just recently, haven't you?" She started weeping and pulled up the sleeves of her long-sleeved dress to show me the vivid scars from the day only two weeks earlier when she had slashed her wrists in an attempt to commit suicide. Right then and there, under the overpowering anointing of God, that young woman was totally delivered from the spirit of suicide and the spirit of lesbianism.

When I went back to that church a year later, I rejoiced to see that this sister was playing a key role on the worship team. She came up to me with a big smile and proudly pulled out a picture and said, "I just want you to know that I got married three weeks ago, and this is the man I married. Now I'm serving the Lord!"

I want you to see the people who are in bondage all around you. They are broken, hurting, and desperate under demonizing influences. Psychologists cannot help them, nor can psychiatrists. God's Word says that this kind won't even come out by a simple command in the name of Jesus Christ—they do not come out except through prayer and fasting. That, my friend, is what the Lord is asking us to do. Are you willing to pay the price to set the captives free? Are you willing to set the captives free in your church, in your neighborhood, and in your city?

> *She was totally delivered from the spirit of suicide and the spirit of lesbianism.*

We shouldn't be satisfied to stop there. There are desperately wicked yokes of bondage choking the people in our inner cities. I want the Church of Jesus Christ to rise up in God's glory. I'm tired of us shooting at each other when there are so many desperate needs out in the world. We are called to set the captives free, and the Lord has given us mighty weapons to pull down the strongholds.

Everyone seeking deliverance from an entangling sin or chronic weakness needs to get desperate. If parents want to see their children healed or set free of demonic oppression, then they need to get desperate for their children. If they are truly humble and desperate before the Lord as they fast for themselves or for their children, then they will often find that it becomes easy to experience or minister deliverance.

WHY DO WE FAST?

I've compiled a list of nine biblical reasons why we fast, and they don't necessarily parallel the list of 12 benefits of fasting listed in Isaiah 58. Many of these points get down to the "nitty gritty" areas of the Christian life, and they answer some of the most common questions I've been asked about fasting over the past two decades.

1. *We fast in obedience to God's Word.*

Fasting is deeply embedded in God's Word. It is a tool of overcoming leaders in both the Old and New Testaments. If the Bible record is any indication, then "Winners fast and losers don't." Here is a very brief sampling of what God has to say to believers, and ministers in particular, about fasting:

> *"Now, therefore," says the Lord, "turn to Me with all your heart, with fasting, with weeping, and with mourning"* (Joel 2:12).

> *But in all things we commend ourselves as ministers of God: in much patience, in tribulations, in needs, in distresses, in stripes, in imprisonments, in tumults, in labors, in sleeplessness, in fastings; by purity, by knowledge, by longsuffering, by kindness, by the Holy Spirit, by sincere love* (2 Corinthians 6:4-6).

> *And Jesus said to them, "Can the friends of the bridegroom mourn as long as the bridegroom is with them? But the days will come when the bridegroom will be taken away from them, and then they will fast"* (Matthew 9:15).

2. *We fast to humble ourselves before God and obtain His grace and power.*

How often do you need grace? Do you need to tap into God's power to accomplish the callings and vision He has placed in your heart? We all need His continuous power to live the victorious Christian life daily. So would it hurt to fast at least one day per week to "keep the plugs clean" in your life? Fasting keeps you honest. James the apostle made this point abundantly clear: If you want power and grace from God, then you have to humble yourself: *"Humble yourselves in the sight of the Lord, and He will lift you up"* (James. 4:10). The Holy Spirit is called the Spirit of grace. If you want the Spirit of grace, if you want the anointing, you humble yourself.

3. *We fast to overcome temptations in areas that keep us from moving into God's power.*

If the anointing is not flowing freely through you, that is a good sign that you need to fast and pray. It is time to clear the channel so God's Spirit can flow through you. Once again, turn to the pattern of the great Pioneer of our faith, Jesus. According to Luke chapter 4, Jesus came out of a wilderness of temptation *in the power of the Spirit.* If you want the same, then do what He did. Jesus ate nothing for 40 days, and afterward the devil came to tempt Him when He was hungry. When Jesus had soundly whipped the devil, He went forth *in power.*

4. *We fast to be purified from sin (and to help others become purified as well).*

According to the Word of God, Jesus Christ took away all the sins of the world on the cross at Calvary. Yet many (if not all) of us have to deal with "besetting" or "entangling" sins that seem to keep popping up again and again. God wants us not only to defeat these entangling sins in our own lives, but also to go beyond our own needs to stand in the gap as intercessors for others. If there is a habit or chronic sin that keeps cropping up in your life, then humble your soul in fasting, and God will purify you. Be prepared, then, for the time the Lord asks you to take upon yourself (through intercession) the sins of others and combine your intercessory prayer with fasting. The great models for this are Jesus Christ and the prophet Daniel:

> *Then I set my face toward the Lord God to make request by prayer and supplications, with fasting, sackcloth, and ashes. And I prayed to the Lord my God, and made confession, and said, "O Lord, great and awesome God, who keeps His covenant and mercy with those who love Him, and with those who keep His commandments, we have sinned and committed iniquity, we have done wickedly and rebelled, even by departing from Your precepts and Your judgments"* (Daniel 9:3-5).

We can pray this great model prayer for ourselves, for our congregation, for our children, and even for our city and nation. It says, "God, we have sinned. We have departed from Your ways, O God. We are in defeat because of our sins and transgressions." Now remember that the man who was praying these things, Daniel, was the most righteous man in his generation! This was the man who would rather pray than escape the lions' den, yet he said, "God, *we* have sinned."

Many times I've shared this principle with pastors who protested, saying, "You don't understand! We are fine. We are OK. We live godly lives here." I tell them, "Listen, you don't understand! We may be OK, but *our cities* and *our nations* are crumbling! We need to take upon ourselves this burden and say, 'God, we have sinned, we have become lazy. Forgive us and restore us.'"

As believers and intercessors in the pattern of the Great Intercessor, we are called and expected to take upon ourselves the burdens of others. It is simply an unavoidable part of "taking up our cross daily." At times, entire cities or nations fast to repent and be purified from sin. This happened in the days of Jonah. The Ninevites were a wicked and violent people who were about to be judged and annihilated by God, but then *they went on a fast* (even the donkeys, camels, and goats were put on a fast!):

> *So the people of Nineveh believed God, proclaimed a fast, and put on sackcloth, from the greatest to the least of them. Then word came to the king of Nineveh; and he arose from his throne and laid aside his robe, covered himself with sackcloth and sat in ashes.*
>
> *And he caused it to be proclaimed and published throughout Nineveh by the decree of the king and his nobles, saying, Let neither man nor beast, herd nor flock, taste anything; do not let them eat, or drink water. But let man and beast be covered with sackcloth, and cry mightily to God; yes, let every one turn from his evil way and from the violence that is in his hands. Who can tell if God will turn and relent, and turn away from His fierce anger, so that we may not perish?*
>
> *Then God saw their works, that they turned from their evil way; and God relented from the disaster that He had said He would bring upon them, and He did not do it* (Jonah 3:5-10).

Fasting for purity can be pretty confusing at times because of the very nature of the cleansing process. Fasting has a way of bringing every nasty habit and irritation you've got just bubbling to the surface. You will quickly notice—especially on longer fasts—that if you have a bad temper hidden down there where no one else (but God and your spouse) can see, then it will come right to the surface and you'll start roaring at people. Be patient and be encouraged, and don't give up. The Lord will clean you out.

5. *We fast to become weak before God so God's power can be strong.*

Fasting is a choice *for God* and *against the flesh*. When you fast, you are making a conscious inward choice demonstrated by an outward act that you want God's power to flow through you, not your own. You want God's answer, not yours.

Many years ago when I was just beginning to step out in the ministry, I received a call from a couple whom I loved and had prayed for often. I didn't have any money to spare at the time, but my heart went out to this couple when they said, "Brother Mahesh, we are in need." They were both in graduate school at the time and they would have to drop out if they didn't find money for tuition somehow or somewhere.

> *Fasting is a choice for God and against the flesh.*

They told me, "Mahesh, we just want you to be in prayer," but I loved them so much that I said, "Well..." and was about to say that I was going to send them all the money I had in my bank account. I was still taking some courses at the university myself, and I needed what money I had managed to save so I could register for my final series of classes. As they talked, I said to myself, "I'm going to take all that I've saved for registration and give it to them." It was the "arm of the flesh" speaking. There's nothing wrong with giving to those in need, but this time they were calling me *to pray* and I was about to simply send them money instead.

Suddenly God seemed to speak to me in the other ear, "Mahesh, do *you* want to help them or would you rather that *I* help them?" I said, "*You*, Sir," and I prayed for them.

The very next day, both of these people received full scholarships to the university. The miracle of provision didn't stop there! God continued to take care of all their needs supernaturally for the next two years! In contrast, the "weak arm of the flesh of Mahesh" could have helped my friends for about three days at best—if I'd totally emptied my slim bank account. God's way is always best. Consider what God's Word has to say:

> *My knees are weak through fasting, and my flesh is feeble from lack of fatness. I also have become a reproach to them; when they look at me, they shake their heads. Help me, O Lord my God! Oh, save me according to Your mercy, That they may know that this is Your hand; that You, Lord, have done it! Let them curse, but You bless...* (Psalm 109:24-28).

> *And He said to me, "My grace is sufficient for you, for My strength is made perfect in weakness." Therefore most gladly I will rather boast in my infirmities, that the power of Christ may rest upon me. Therefore I take pleasure in infirmities, in reproaches, in needs, in persecutions, in distresses, for Christ's sake. For when I am weak, then I am strong* (2 Corinthians 12:9-10).

I've learned that it is important for us as ministers of God to become completely weak before God. It is at that point that the Lord will send us out in His power.

6. *We fast to obtain God's support in order to accomplish His will.*

The leaders at the church in Antioch fasted and prayed before they sent out Barnabas and Paul. This was done so the leaders would make the right choice, and it was done to ensure their success in the gospel mission. Barnabas and Paul followed the same pattern in the foreign cities where they established churches—they fasted and prayed before appointing elders in those cities. The fasting and prayer helped guide their choices and helped ensure the successful ministry of those elders. They wanted God's support to continue in those churches long after the apostles had gone (see Acts 13:3-4; 14:23).

7. *We fast in times of crisis.*

Men and women have always turned to God in prayer and fasting in times of crisis. The Book of Esther records what was probably the most critical time in the history of the Jewish nation. Even though Hitler brutally massacred six million Jews during World War II in a terrible holocaust, thousands of Jews still survived in other places around the world. In Esther's time, the Jews had not yet been dispersed and Haman was actually on the verge of successfully destroying the *entire* Jewish race! The king of the Persians and Medes had already signed the death warrant when Esther commanded the Jews to observe a fast before she risked her life to enter the king's presence to obtain mercy and pardon for her people.

> *Then Esther told them to reply to Mordecai: "Go, gather all the Jews who are present in Shushan, and fast for me; neither eat nor drink for three days, night or day. My maids and I will fast likewise. And so I will go to the king, which is against the law; and if I perish, I perish!"* (Esther 4:15-16)

In times of crisis, we may need to fast the most aggressive fast of all and totally abstain from food and water. However, I would never counsel you to do that for more than *three days* unless you are in the literal glory and presence of God. This three-day fast is the fast that Esther asked the Jews to observe. In the end, God turned that crisis around and brought deliverance to all the Jews.

Again in Second Chronicles 20, Judah was about to be destroyed by enemies when King Jehoshaphat put the people on a fast. In the end, they witnessed one of the most dramatic acts of supernatural deliverance recorded in the Bible as the angels of God came and wiped out the armies of three invading nations!

8. *We fast when seeking God's direction.*

> *Then I proclaimed a fast there at the river of Ahava, that we might humble ourselves before our God, to seek from Him the right way for us and our little ones and all our possessions. For I was ashamed to request of the king an escort of soldiers and horsemen to help us against the enemy on the road, because we had spoken to the king, saying, "The hand of our God is upon all those for good who seek Him, but His power and His wrath are against all those who forsake Him." So we fasted and entreated our God for this, and He answered our prayer* (Ezra 8:21-23).

When you need God's direction, when you are confused about which way to go, one of the best things you can do is *fast*. This is especially true in the sometimes confusing area of personal relationships, particularly for those believers trying to make a choice about whom to marry. The Lord taught me this principle of fasting before I got married, and I fasted for my wife even though I was not yet married and didn't even know her! I knew that God had not called me to live alone, and I knew that God knew where and who she was; so I fasted and prayed for her. Bonnie and I compared notes later on and discovered that at the most critical time in her life, after her parents got a divorce, she went through some very intense times. That was the time period when I was fasting for her and praying that God would give her deliverance!

9.   *We fast for understanding and divine revelation.*

As believers, we need more than direction. We need *revelation* and *understanding* of certain matters, situations, or truths in the Bible. The Bible says, *"You go, therefore, and read from the scroll which you have written at my instruction, the words of the Lord, in the hearing of the people in the Lord's house on the day of fasting..."* (Jer. 36:6).

Sometimes the Lord's revelation doesn't necessarily come at the time of the fast, but later on. This happened to me the time the Lord showed me a *wonderful principle of healing* during a mass crusade in Haiti. The meetings were held immediately after the Duvalier regime fell in that nation, and God had given us some wonderful miracles in the services. However, the local voodoo priests and witch doctors had become so disturbed by our crusade that for the first time ever they issued a nationwide radio broadcast calling for a meeting between all the voodoo priests and practitioners to put curses on us! I said, "Wow, wonderful! Let's see what you can do." (I responded in this way because like Elijah before me, I *knew* God was surrounding us with His glory.)

> *I knew God was surrounding us with His glory.*

During this same series of meetings, a certain woman who had been born blind was brought to the front by her granddaughter. Each time this little lady would come to the front with her hand on her granddaughter's shoulder, and I would pray for her. Every time the anointing of God would hit her and she would fall down like I had hit her with all my strength, although I barely touched her. I knew something had happened, but each time I helped her up and asked, "How are you, Grandma?" she would blink her still blind eyes and say, "I can't see." I could only answer, "OK. Come again."

The same thing happened each service after that for seven days and nights. She would be led forward by her granddaughter. The power of God would hit her, her body would shake, and down she would go. I knew it was the genuine power of the Lord hitting her. It was so obvious that I almost wanted the Lord to be gentle. Yet each time I helped her up again and asked, "How are you?" she would shake her head and say she still couldn't see.

I was really struggling with this situation. As you might imagine, when you are conducting healing services, you don't necessarily want the first people to come up for prayer to be born blind! There's a strong temptation to ask for the warts or headaches first. The Lord doesn't think that way.

By the fourth day, I was getting tired of seeing Grandma coming forward for prayer. Thank God she wasn't looking to me for healing, she was looking to the Lord. Once again, the same thing happened. In fact, the *same thing happened* on the fifth day and the sixth day. She would come forward, I would pray, she would fall down, I would help her up, she would shake her head no, and I would say, "God bless you, come back again," and so on.

On the last service of the last day of the crusade in Haiti, my favorite grandmother came forward to the front once again with her hand on her granddaughter's shoulder. Once again I prayed for her, and again the incredible power of God hit her so hard that she was absolutely knocked to the floor, just like every service before that. Once again I knelt down and said, "God bless you, Grandma," and went on. But this time the Lord said, "Help her up." So I said, "OK." I went back to help this dear lady to her feet.

Once again I asked her, "How are you, Grandma?" She blinked her eyes and said, *"I can see you clearly!"* God had totally recreated her eyes and given her sight for the first time in her life! Outwardly I exclaimed, "How wonderful!" but inwardly I said, *You know, Lord, You could have done this the first day!*

Many months later during an extended time of fasting and prayer, I was driving down a street in South Florida where I lived at the time. I was minding my own business and wasn't even praying on the eighteenth day of the fast when suddenly, right in front of my eyes, I began to view scenes of the times I had prayed for that precious Haitian grandmother. It was almost as if I was watching a full-color videotape of those prayer times.

> *Don't get discouraged. Keep praying until you see healing and deliverance!*

I had wondered many times about the seven days I had prayed for that blind woman, and suddenly I found myself reliving those times in living color. Only this time I knew I was seeing through the eyes of the Spirit. As this woman came up for prayer in each service, the Lord showed me that there was a creature that looked similar to an octopus with several tentacles wrapped around the woman's eyes. Every time I prayed, the anointing of God would hit her and knock off one of the tentacles.

During the second prayer, a second tentacle was supernaturally removed. During the third prayer, a third tentacle came off. Finally, on the last night in the last service, the woman came forward with a single tentacle still wrapped around her eyes. It was like a spirit of blindness, the main demon that had kept her bound in a world of darkness. When I prayed for her the last day, the last tentacle came off and she could see clearly.

The Lord revealed to me that at times, demonic obstructions hold us or cling to us with several arms. Every time you pray under the anointing, *something happens*. You can count on that. The Lord says to many of us, "Don't get discouraged. Keep praying through until the last tentacle comes off and you see the healing and deliverance!"

About Mahesh Chavda

Mahesh Chavda is the founder and senior pastor of All Nations Church in Charlotte, North Carolina. An international evangelist, Mahesh and his wife, Bonnie, have led more than 700,000 people to Christ around the globe. They also oversee the worldwide "Watch of the Lord" prayer movement and conduct training conferences that teach Christians to do the works of Jesus and to move in the anointing of the Holy Spirit. The Chavdas and their four children reside in Charlotte, North Carolina.

Chapter 9

PRAYER CAN BE
POWERFUL
(OR OTHERWISE)

by C. Peter Wagner

You ask and do not receive, because
you ask amiss... (James 4:3).

The name of the church is The Prayer Cave. When Pastor Thomas Muthee founded the church in the small city of Kiambu not long ago, prayer had played such a vital role for him that calling it "The Prayer Cave" was a natural. (This might seem like an odd name to the ears of most American believers. All across Kenya, however, the most prominent nation of East Africa, creativity reigns in assigning church names.)

No other church I am aware of better exemplifies what this chapter is all about—praying with power. I think it is important for us to understand that prayer is not some ethereal exercise that has little measurable effect on the real world in which we live. I know of no better way to begin to understand how powerful prayer can be than to explore a concrete example such as The Prayer Cave in Kiambu, Kenya. I will tell you more soon.

Prayer Truly Works

Meanwhile, a central thesis underlying all my writings about prayer is that prayer works. Not all prayer works, but effective prayer does. Powerful prayer works. I have emphasized those adjectives to highlight what many of us already know in our hearts, but sometimes hesitate to admit—not all prayer is equal. Just as some prayer is effective, so some is ineffective, and some is in between. Just as some prayer is powerful, so, unfortunately, some is equally impotent. I am enough of a born pragmatist to have virtually no incentive to write a series of books about prayer in general. My interest is almost exclusively in powerful prayer, not in the other kinds.

The essence of prayer is a personal relationship between a believer and God. Some call it "intimacy with the Father." This is true, and it is important. For this reason it would not be correct to say that any believing prayer is bad per se. I would not want to make a distinction between good prayer and bad prayer, for example. Some prayer, however, we must admit, can be misguided and therefore lack the power it could have. James says, *"You ask and do not receive, because you ask amiss..."* (James 4:3). Wrong motives can weaken prayer, as can sin in our lives and many other things I will mention from time to time as we move on.

The distinction I am making is, more accurately, between good prayer and better prayer. My wife, Doris, likes to say, "No prayer is wasted." All good prayer can be seen as a step in the right direction, but some of those steps may be smaller than they need to be. If you are reading this book, the odds are high that you have a burning desire in your heart to pray more powerfully than you ordinarily have been doing. You may be on a relatively low level right now, but you do not want to stay there. You may be on a high level of prayer power, but you know that there are higher levels yet, and that is where you want to be.

MEASURING THE POWER OF PRAYER

How will you know when you reach a higher level of prayer? One way is to see an increase in concrete, measurable answers to your prayers. That is why I like to assert that prayer works. James does not say, *"the prayer of a righteous man avails much."* *He seems to go out of his way to say that "the effective, fervent prayer of a righteous [person] avails much"* (James 5:16, emphasis added). If he had left it at that point, the statement would certainly have been true, although somewhat vague. To avoid this, James immediately goes on to make it more concrete. He uses Elijah, a human being just like us, as his example. Elijah prayed that it would not rain, and it did not. Then he prayed that it would rain, and it did. Elijah's prayers worked! (See James 5:17-18.)

I wish all my prayers would be like Elijah's. I must confess, however, that I have not arrived at Elijah's level—yet. I am not even at the level of many of my closest friends—yet. One thing I do know is that I am on a higher level than I was last year, and that next year I intend, with God's help, to be higher than I am now. I may never reach Elijah's level, but it is not because such a thing is impossible.

In the passage I am citing, James takes pains to point out that *"Elijah was a man with a nature like ours"* (James 5:17). It is certainly possible that God could use you and that He could use me the way He used Elijah. Why not? That is exactly what I desire. I want my prayers to be more effective in the future than they have been in the past.

I have no doubt that what follows will help your prayers become more powerful than they have been in the past. Just feeling the pulse of a dynamic church such as The Prayer Cave will fill you with renewed faith and hope for effective prayer in your personal life, in the lives of your family, in your church, and in your community. I think you will agree with me that Pastor Thomas Muthee is fairly close to the Elijah level.

THE KENYA PRAYER CAVE

Pastor Thomas Muthee is a valued personal friend. He is my East African director of the International Spiritual Warfare Network. He is a clear thinker, articulate, wise, and respected by his peers in Africa and other parts of the world.

I say this, not to inflate my friend Thomas, but simply to assure the readers that we are not talking about some obscure flake, but about a church leader of good reputation and high integrity.

As a side note, I am deeply grateful to my colleague, George Otis Jr. of The Sentinel Group, for introducing me to Pastor Thomas Muthee and for interviewing him to collect details of this remarkable story. The following story is paraphrased from George Otis Jr.'s book, *The Twilight Labyrinth*.[1]

Thomas Muthee would be commonly identified as a mega-church pastor. The Prayer Cave church is growing rapidly and, at this writing, approaching 4,000 members, or 5 percent of Kiambu's population of 80,000. Almost all the members are new converts because very few residents of Kiambu were Christians when Thomas arrived. How did this church grow so vigorously, and how did it come to have such a measurable influence on the whole city?

Without any hesitation whatsoever, Thomas Muthee would say that it happened through powerful prayer.

Thomas and his wife had returned to Kenya from a time in Scotland. He was ministering as an itinerant evangelist, and his wife was teaching school. While in prayer one day, he heard the Lord say to him, "I want you to plant a church in Kiambu."

(Hearing from the Lord in prayer was not a new experience for Thomas, although it would be for many Christians whom I know. This is such a vital component of powerful prayer that I have dedicated an entire chapter to the subject of two-way prayer in my book, *Praying With Power.*)

After spending a good deal more time with the Lord and testing the word with his wife and others—always a good safe-guard—Thomas was certain this was indeed the command of God for a new career and for a new place of residence. There was no question in his mind that he had to obey. Thomas, however, did not look forward to the assignment with one bit of pleasure.

A Murder Capital and a Preacher's Graveyard

Only a few miles distant from the beautiful capital city of Nairobi, Kiambu had gained a national reputation for having the worst crime, violence, drunkenness, immorality, thievery, and human degradation. Public disorder was the rule, and loud rock music was blaring from speakers in front of barrooms through-out the nights. It was the murder capital of Kenya, registering up to eight killings in a given month. The economy of the city was so bad that government officials reportedly paid bribes to their superiors so as not to be assigned to Kiambu.

A cloud of mystery also hung over the city. Everyone there knew that in one certain place many, and often unexplainable, automobile accidents regularly occurred. It was considered a good month when as few as three fatalities were reported as a result of traffic accidents. Stranger still was the fact that no matter how mangled the bodies of the accident victims were, to all intents and purposes, no bleeding occurred—ever! At times, some reported hearing screeching tires and crashing metal, but when they ran to the site, no cars could be seen at all!

Although he had never visited Kiambu, Thomas knew its reputation well, and he did not like the city, much less the prospects of making his home there. Add to that the fact that, although he had been in Christian ministry for years, he had never contemplated planting a new church. He believed he had the gift of an evangelist, and he was using it successfully as he traveled around the nation.

Even if he had intended to plant a church, Kiambu would have been Thomas' last choice as a likely site because the city had also gained the reputation as a preacher's graveyard. Pastor after pastor tried to plant a church there and soon left defeated and discouraged. The Pentecostal/Charismatic kind of churches, which were growing vigorously in other parts of Kenya, could not seem to grow either in Kiambu. The largest, pastored by a wonderful, dedicated man of God, had grown to less than 60 members after 15 years of faithful ministry! Another, also 15 years old, had 40 members, and another only 30.

Six Months of Prayer and Fasting

The assignment was clear; but how to implement it? If Thomas had taken my course at Fuller in church planting, he might have conducted demographic surveys, feasibility studies, public opinion polls, and cost analyses studies. Not that any of these are bad—I continue to recommend them highly to the best of intelligent church planters. God, however, gave Thomas a different strategy few church planters have used, but in this case it was probably the one way a city as engulfed by spiritual darkness as Kiambu could be penetrated to any significant degree by the gospel.

By mentioning this, I do not want to leave the impression that I am suggesting Thomas Muthee's method should be substituted for tried-and-true church growth and church-planting principles. I definitely do, however, want to leave the impression that church planters of any stripe would do well to take a close look at what Thomas did, discern the spiritual principles behind his activities, and, although they decide not to copy his method, at least consider employing the principles.

God's plan for Thomas and his wife was for them to pray and fast for six months, which they faithfully did. Thomas did not so much as visit Kiambu, only 10 miles from his home, during that time period. They practiced a variety of fasts during those months, sometimes fasting a meal or two, sometimes for extended periods, drinking juice or water only, as well as some absolute fasts when they consumed no food or drink.

I personally heard Thomas describe this season of waiting on the Lord. He saw it as proactive spiritual warfare. He said, "If we are going to win the battle for Kiambu, we must win it in the air. The ground troops must not invade the territory of the enemy without first achieving victory in the invisible world. I would not want to step my foot into Kiambu until the spiritual forces of darkness over the city have lost their grip."

Thomas was no stranger to the devices of satan. He was an experienced intercessor, and in his evangelistic work he had confronted the enemy in power encounters on a variety of levels. He had learned that the devil assigns certain specific demons over towns, cities, and nations, as well as families. He said, "Over this extended time of prayer and fasting, I wanted to know exactly what was keeping Kiambu so politically, socially, economically, and spiritually oppressed."

The term many of us are using for the quest that was engaging Thomas Muthee at the time is "spiritual mapping." The major purpose of spiritual mapping is to target our prayers as accurately as possible. As Thomas prayed, he found himself asking more and more for the exact identity of the major principality over the city. As I often say, it is not necessary to know the name of the chief spirit to pray effectively for a city such as Kiambu, but if God chooses to reveal the name, it is an advantage. In this case, Thomas believed he should ask specifically for the name.

THE POWER OVER THE CITY: WITCHCRAFT

God answered, this time through a vision. In the vision, Thomas clearly saw the principality over Kiambu, and its name was "Witchcraft." He also saw many other demons around Witchcraft and under its command. From that point onward, the prayers of Thomas and his wife were much more specifically targeted, and they sensed in the Spirit that considerable damage was being done in the invisible world to the dark angels that had enjoyed such a free reign over Kiambu for generations.

The name they received was a functional name—a spirit of witchcraft. That demon might well have also had a proper name, similar to some we read about in the Bible such as "Wormwood" or "Abaddon" or "Beelzebub," but in this instance Thomas apparently did not need to know what it was. If he needed it, God would undoubtedly have revealed it to him. At the same time, the vision was so clear that Thomas assigned the proper name, "Witchcraft," to the spirit who was controlling that activity and thereby influencing much of what was happening in the city.

At the end of the six months of prayer and fasting, Thomas felt peace in his heart and mind. He sensed that the major phase of the ministry to reach Kiambu with the gospel had been completed. He saw in the Spirit that the spiritual atmosphere over

Kiambu had been sufficiently cleared through powerful prayer and that the forces of darkness over the city were losing their stranglehold on the city and were now in disarray. It was time for the ground forces to move into enemy territory.

INVASION: BY AN ARMY OF TWO!

The ground forces consisted of only two people—Thomas and his wife. When they moved there, though, they discovered that the way had been prepared so well that they were the first Christian ministers allowed to use the Kiambu municipal hall to preach the gospel.

Their strategy was to win people through public evangelistic meetings, so Thomas, drawing on his extensive experience as an evangelist, began the meetings in January 1989. One of the first things he did was to borrow some used tires from a local mechanic, because Thomas is very short.

He piled them up, fashioned a platform, preached the Word, and saw eight people saved the first night!

> *What is gained by prayer must be maintained by prayer!*

The evangelistic harvest continued, and the new church met in the municipal hall for more than a year. Thomas became more and more dissatisfied, though, because they could not pray as he wanted on site. They had use of the building on Sundays and on Wednesday nights only. Thomas' vision was that his church facility should be used for prayer 24 hours a day, every day. He knew well what I have heard many intercessors say, "What is gained by prayer must be maintained by prayer!" He was convinced that if his new church was to continue to grow and ultimately have an influence on the whole city of Kiambu, prayer had to be the most prominent ongoing component of his philosophy of ministry.

Soon they were able to move out of the municipal hall, but only into the basement of another building. It might have been rather dark and dingy, but from the day they moved in, the 24-hour prayer has never stopped! Going into the basement felt something like going into a cave, so people naturally began referring to it as The Prayer Cave, and the name stuck. The church, as might be expected, has a more official name (Word of Faith Church), but it is known far and wide only as The Kiambu Prayer Cave, although it no longer meets in the basement.

The Spiritual Counterattack

The way I am narrating this case study might sound as if the first couple of years of The Prayer Cave were a piece of cake—no problems, no heartaches, no setbacks. On the contrary, the spiritual counterattack was fierce. Thomas soon discovered that the human being whom the principality over the city, Witchcraft, was using the most was a notorious sorcerer named "Mama Jane." She did her witchcraft and fortune-telling in a place she had perversely named "Emmanuel Clinic." She was considered by many as the most powerful person in the city, and both politicians and businesspeople frequented Emmanuel Clinic to have their fortunes told and to receive Mama Jane's blessing.

One more thing—the Emmanuel Clinic happened to be located near an open market and precisely at that part of the city where the mysterious fatal traffic accidents had been occurring month after month!

Every Saturday night Mama Jane went to Thomas' church site, performed magic, and cast her spells and curses. She let it be known to the city officials that she could not help them with her fortune-telling as much as she used to because this new church seemed to be "cutting her lines of communication." Consequently, one of the outcomes was that not only the city authorities, but also the pastors of other Christian churches began attacking the ministry of The Prayer Cave. That part of it was no fun!

Thomas Muthee and the church members, praying 24 hours a day, did what they could to counteract the demonic attacks against the church. Some Christian leaders seem to think that Christians are immune to satan's attacks. They trivialize the devil by calling him a "toothless lion." Such an attitude of denial only plays into satan's hands and gives him free rein to continue his plans "to kill, steal and destroy" (John 10:10). Such was not the case with the members of The Prayer Cave. They knew well that Mama Jane's counterattack was real, it was powerful, and it was doing considerable damage to the cause of Christ. The Christians, day after day, cried out to God for more power.

WAS MAMA JANE'S SORCERY TOO MUCH?

God answered by bringing Thomas Muthee and his congregation to a place of desperation. The power of evil had invaded the church to the point that they could hardly pray. One day it got so bad that they started a worship song and were never able to finish it! Something was going on! They went outside and found the remains of fresh places of sacrifices and rituals left behind by Mama Jane.

After that, Thomas Muthee went before the Lord, crying in agony. Was this work going to fail? Was Kiambu truly a graveyard of pastors? Would his spiritual tombstone be added to the others? By this time, Muthee was thoroughly convinced that the demonic powers entrusted to Mama Jane had been the very forces that had driven pastor after pastor out of Kiambu.

"God," he prayed, "Do not let me be the next to go—show me the way forward!"

God answered this prayer in a still, small voice by simply suggesting, "My son, I want you to get intercessors on the job."

Fortunately, Thomas understood what God meant. He realized that although he had a congregation of many, many pray-ers, he had not recognized, designated, empowered, and released intercessors. Just as all Christians are expected to be witnesses for Christ and of them only a few are chosen by God to be evangelists, so all Christians are expected to be pray-ers, but only a few of them are chosen to be intercessors. This is another one of those important components of a full-orbed prayer ministry I have included in Chapter 7 of my book *Praying With Power*.

Not wanting to make a mistake or stretch the time line, Thomas came right to the point and said, "Lord, I am ready to do it. Who are the intercessors You have chosen?" Remarkably, God immediately answered and told him five intercessors had been selected at the present time. He also gave Thomas their names!

One approach might have been to bring the five together to fast and pray once a week. A much more radical strategy seemed to be called for, though. Thomas assigned each intercessor to fast and pray for a whole day, then another for the next day and so on. That way, one of the intercessors was always fasting and praying.

Intercessors Need Armor Bearers

The initial results seemed to be positive, but the intercessors began suffering serious attacks. On their designated fasting days, sickness and other things debilitated them and prevented their prayers from being as powerful as they should be. Pastor Thomas asked the Lord to reveal what should be done, and God took him to the biblical story of Jonathan, who, unlike King Saul, went to war having an armor bearer at his side. Through this

seemingly trivial detail, God showed Thomas that each intercessor needed armor bearers on the specific day designated for
fasting and praying.

Thomas called together his intercessors, who by then had
grown to a team of nine, and told them that each person who
was designated to fast on a particular day would be covered by
two armor bearers. One would be the person who had fasted and
prayed the day before, and the other would be the one who was
scheduled to fast and pray the following day. These two would
form a protective hedge of prayer around the one on duty.

They did it, and it worked! The spiritual harassment suddenly stopped. The armor-bearer plan has been in place ever
since, and at this writing the intercession team has grown to 400
highly-committed individuals. Instead of only one intercessor
fasting and praying each day, they are now divided into blocks
of 15 or 20, which means that every single day either 15 or 20 are
praying and have a prayer shield spread over each one by two
other intercessors.

In Thomas Muthee's opinion, adding the serious intercessors to the prayer ministry of The Prayer Cave was the decisive
turning point in the spiritual battle for Kiambu. An increasing
number of Mama Jane's clients were becoming Christians and
publicly burning the charms and fetishes she had sold them.
The way was now open for Muthee to issue a public ultimatum:
"Mama Jane either gets saved and serves the Lord or she leaves
town! There is no longer room in Kiambu for both of us!" In plain
terms, Thomas Muthee had challenged Mama Jane to a power
encounter, much as Elijah had challenged the priests of Baal.

THE POWER ENCOUNTER

By now the word was spreading around to the city officials
that Mama Jane did not seem to have the power she used to have.

Her clients were embarrassing her by openly burning fetishes and renouncing curses. Some began pointing out that it could be no coincidence that her Emmanuel Clinic was right next to the area where the serious accidents were occurring. The whole process was brought to a climax when three young children were killed in one of the mysterious accidents. The people of the city were furious. They suspected that it was Mama Jane's black magic that was causing the accidents. They wanted to stone her!

The police were called in, and they entered Mama Jane's house to investigate. In one room of the house they were startled to find one of the largest pythons they had ever seen. They immediately shot the snake and killed it. That natural act caused the spiritual battle to end. Mama Jane was taken by the police for questioning and was later released. She quickly and wisely opted to leave town for good. Instead of a preacher's graveyard, Kiambu had miraculously been transformed to a witch's graveyard!

Let's not lose the significance of the snake. That was the event in the visible world that reflected what had been happening in the invisible world. Before he had arrived in Kiambu, Thomas Muthee had been informed by God that Witchcraft was the principality ruling the city, supported by any number of lesser spirits. Witchcraft's human vehicle was the witch, Mama Jane, who had blasphemed God by calling her den of iniquity "Emmanuel Clinic." She had also become the most powerful woman in Kiambu.

When the apostle Paul arrived in Philippi, he encountered a similar situation. The most spiritually-powerful woman in Philippi was a slave girl *"possessed with a spirit of divination* [or witchcraft]" (Acts 16:16). The details were different, but after a time, Paul also provoked a power encounter and said to the spirit, "I command you in the name of Jesus Christ to come out of her" (v. 18). The slave girl immediately lost her magical powers, many miracles took place, and a strong church was planted in Philippi.

What about the snake? Most of our translations use the phrase "spirit of divination" or "spirit of clairvoyance," which is the functional name of the territorial spirit over Philippi. Biblical scholars, however, tell us that a more literal rendering of the Greek would give the spirit a proper name. For example, Simon Kistemaker points out that the best way to translate the Greek is "a spirit, namely a Python."[2]

Here is one indication of the relationship of the snake in the visible world to spirits of witchcraft in the invisible world. It is common that in art designed to glorify the demonic, snakes are frequently used to represent witchcraft.

It comes as no surprise, then, to those familiar with spiritual warfare and spiritual mapping that a huge python was found in Mama Jane's house, and that killing the snake was the final blow to her evil power in Kiambu.

POWERFUL PRAYER CAN CHANGE A CITY!

The point I am trying to make in this chapter is that powerful prayer works. Our case study of The Prayer Cave is a convincing example. The spiritual defeat of Mama Jane is convincing enough, but that is not all. What effect did the prayer ministry of The Prayer Cave have on the city of Kiambu as a whole?

When Mama Jane left the city, things began to change quickly and dramatically. The unbelievers in the city also recognized the cause-and-effect relationship between the power encounter and the subsequent changes in the community.

Economically, the city is now prosperous. Government officials, instead of allegedly paying bribes so as not to be assigned to Kiambu, now are said to pay bribes to get the assignment.

The crime and violence associated with the city in the national media is now virtually gone. The chief of police has recently visited Pastor Muthee and told him that because of what he has done to Kiambu, he has been granted permission to preach anywhere at any time; he can use any volume on the loudspeakers and does not need a permit. Some of the most notorious criminals of the city are now saved and are members of The Prayer Cave. One of the worst drug dealers has renounced such behavior and is enrolled in the church Bible school; he plays bass guitar in the worship team, and he uses his spare time to evangelize patients in the hospitals.

Alcoholism is notably diminished in Kiambu. The intercessors went on prayerwalks around the barrooms, and the loud music is a thing of the past. One of the most prominent high-volume discos is now a church! A small valley near the city had been notorious as a den of bootleggers, producing and selling native beer on the black market. The intercessors targeted it for prayerwalking. The still is now closed, and The Prayer Cave has purchased the land to build its new church facility!

> *Do not forget the central cause of the awesome changes in the city of Kiambu, Kenya— powerful prayer.*

What about the mysterious automobile accidents? As you might have guessed, no such accidents have occurred since the day on which the symbolic python was destroyed. Witchcraft was defeated!

Finally the Kingdom of God is coming to Kiambu. No more hostility is present among Christian pastors. Repentance and reconciliation is the order of the day. Churches of all denominations across the city are now growing rapidly, the same as they have in other parts of Kenya. Pastors regularly eat together and pray together. At this writing, they are making plans for the first joint evangelistic citywide crusade that Kiambu has ever known.

PRAYER POWER IN ARGENTINA

Mama Jane got off easily, compared to two cases of powerful prayer in Argentina. My wife, Doris, and I have been working with Ed Silvoso, author of *That None Should Perish* (Regal Books), in Argentina for many years. The first season of ministry was in the city of Resistencia in northern Argentina. One of the territorial spirits that had Resistencia under its control was San La Muerte, the spirit of death. Multitudes worshiped this spirit because it promised them "a good death."

Think of the desperation and hopelessness that must have been present in the hearts of those people to grasp hold of such a promise! Death was worshiped in 13 shrines around the city. Many people would take one of its images, carved from human bone, and have it surgically implanted under their skin so that no matter where they went they would be assured of a good death!

A great deal of fervent prayer began to be offered in Resistencia after seminars about intercession were taught by Doris, Cindy Jacobs, Argentine Pastor Eduardo Lorenzo, and others. When the time came for the climactic evangelistic event, Doris and Cindy flew to Resistencia and were met with a startling piece of news. The week before they arrived, the high priestess of the cult of San La Muerte had been smoking in bed. She fell asleep, her bed caught on fire, and only three things were consumed by the flames: her mattress, herself, and her statue of San La Muerte, which was in another room! Nothing else in the house was touched. The one who had promised others a good death had died a horrible death herself!

Needless to say, the harvest was great in Resistencia. In a short time, the number of believers there had increased by 102 percent! The spirit of death was defeated by powerful prayer, and the Kingdom of God poured through Resistencia.

CONFRONTING WITCHCRAFT IN MAR DEL PLATA

The other incident in Argentina took place in the resort city of Mar del Plata. After careful planning and painstaking spiritual mapping, Doris, Cindy, Eduardo Lorenzo, and others felt led to take a team of local pastors and intercessors to pray in the central plaza of the city after conducting a prayer and spiritual warfare seminar. They prayed for a couple of hours, asking God to break the spiritual strongholds there. As they were praying out loud, specifically against the spirit of witchcraft, which they had discerned was the major principality over the city, several noticed that the bells in the cathedral rang for a considerable period of time at exactly 4 P.M.

The news did not reach them until the next day, when they heard from one of the pastors who had attended the seminar but felt led to pray at home rather than go to the plaza. This pastor's home happened to be right across the street from the home of a Macumba witch of Mar del Plata, the one who had boasted of joining other witches in launching spiritual attacks against the Christian pastors of the city. Shortly after 4 p.m., the pastor saw an ambulance pull up to the witch's house and carry her away, dead. She had been in fine health, but witnesses said that she suddenly dropped dead at 4 p.m. for no apparent cause!

Cindy Jacobs comments about the incident: "We were stunned when we heard this report. While we were not happy that the woman had died, we were acutely aware that God was sending a clear message of judgment against witchcraft."[3]

WHY DOES PRAYER MAKE A DIFFERENCE?

In the case in Mar del Plata, the attitude of God against witchcraft had not been changed by the prayer action in the plaza. Had it not been for the prayer, however, witchcraft in Mar del Plata would have been business as usual, at least according to my best understanding of the theology of prayer. The prayer in the plaza was targeted, it was aggressive, it was empowered by the Holy Spirit, and it was intentional. It was an Elijah kind of prayer. Exactly the same thing could be said about the prayer in Resistencia and in Kiambu, Kenya. In each case, prayer moved the hand of God to show His power in the visible world. Although prayer did not change God's attitude, it did influence His actions.

How does the prayer action of human beings relate to the sovereignty of God? This is a key issue in understanding the difference between prayer in general and effective, fervent prayer.

When I was first moving deeply into my study and understanding of prayer some years ago, one of the statements that helped me most was a chapter title in Jack Hayford's book *Prayer Is Invading the Impossible:* "If We Don't, He Won't." Jack Hayford did not say, "If we don't, He can't." That would have been terrible theology. God is sovereign, and He can do anything He wants to do. The sovereign God, however, apparently has chosen to order His creation in such a way that many of His actions are contingent on the prayers of His people. It is as if God has a Plan A He will implement if believers pray. If they do not, He has a Plan B. Plan A is obviously better for all concerned than Plan B. The choice, according to God's design, is ours. If we choose to pray and if we pray powerfully, more blessing will come and God's Kingdom will be manifested here on earth in a more glorious way than if we choose not to.

I love the way one of the great scholars of prayer of our generation, Richard Foster, puts it, "We are working with God to determine the future. Certain things will happen in history if we pray rightly."[4]

Any who might doubt this need only ask Thomas Muthee or Cindy Jacobs or, for that matter Mama Jane, to dispel doubts and to build faith that powerful prayer can, indeed, determine the history of our cities and nations.

About C. Peter Wagner

C. Peter Wagner serves as Founding President of Global Harvest Ministries and Chancellor of Wagner Leadership Institute. Wagner's apostolic ministry convenes strategic groups of apostles, prophets, deliverance ministers, and educators on a regular basis. Peter and Doris Wagner served as field missionaries in Bolivia from 1956 to 1971. From 1971 to 2001, he taught church growth in the Fuller Theological Seminary School of World Mission. He is the author of over 70 published works. He and Doris make their home in Colorado Springs and have three children, nine grandchildren, and three great-grandchildren.

ENDNOTES

1. George Otis Jr., *The Twilight Labyrinth* (Grand Rapids, MI: Chosen Books, 1997).

2. Simon J. Kistemaker, *Exposition of the Acts of the Apostles* (Grand Rapids, MI: Baker Book House, 1990), 594.

3. Cindy Jacobs, *Possessing the Gates of the Enemy* (Grand Rapids, MI: Baker Book House, 1991; rev. ed. 1994), 103.

4. Richard Foster, *Celebration of Discipline* (San Francisco, CA: HarperSanFrancisco, 1988), 35.

IN THE RIGHT HANDS, THIS BOOK WILL CHANGE LIVES!

Most of the people who need this message will not be looking for this book. To change their lives, you need to put a copy of this book in their hands.

> *But others (seeds) fell into good ground, and brought forth fruit, some a hundred-fold, some sixty-fold, some thirty-fold* (Matthew 13:8).

Our ministry is constantly seeking methods to find the good ground, the people who need this anointed message to change their lives. Will you help us reach these people?

> *Remember this—a farmer who plants only a few seeds will get a small crop. But the one who plants generously will get a generous crop* (2 Corinthians 9:6).

EXTEND THIS MINISTRY BY SOWING
3 BOOKS, 5 BOOKS, 10 BOOKS, OR MORE TODAY,
AND BECOME A LIFE CHANGER!

Thank you,

Don Nori Sr., Founder
Destiny Image
Since 1982